MAHĀBHĀRATA UNRAVELLED II

MAHĀBHĀRATA UNRAVELLED II

The Dharma Discourses

AMI GANATRA

BLOOMSBURY
NEW DELHI • LONDON • OXFORD • NEW YORK • SYDNEY

BLOOMSBURY INDIA
Bloomsbury Publishing India Pvt. Ltd
Second Floor, LSC Building No. 4, DDA Complex, Pocket C – 6 & 7,
Vasant Kunj, New Delhi, 110070

BLOOMSBURY, BLOOMSBURY INDIA and the Diana logo
are trademarks of Bloomsbury Publishing Plc

First published in India 2024
This edition published 2024

ISBN: PB: 978-93-56409-33-0; eBook: 978-93-56407-20-6
4 6 8 10 11 9 7 5

Typeset in Adobe Caslon Pro by Manipal Technologies Limited
Printed and bound in India by Gopsons Papers Pvt. Ltd., Noida

MIX
Paper | Supporting responsible forestry
FSC www.fsc.org FSC® C191020

To

Maharshi Vyāsa and the Rishi paramparā

Maa

Mila, Ravi, Maya

त्वदीयं वस्तु गोविन्दः तुभ्यमेव समर्पये !

CONTENTS

Introduction

In my first book, *Mahābhārata Unravelled: Lesser-Known Facets of a Well-Known History*, I covered the life stories, the itihāsa, of our ancestors as narrated by Rishi Veda Vyāsa. But the Mahābhārata is more than just a story of the past. Tradition accords it the status of a Dharmashāstra.

What Are Dharmashāstras?

Dharmashāstras are texts that provide guidance about the social code of conduct for various groups of people. They provide guidance about personal and social ethics, social norms for interactions, roles and responsibilities of the rulers and the prajā (citizens/subjects) as well as their religious duties, different aspects of jurisprudence and other such matters. The main objective of these texts was to guide the king and the administrators to establish a dharmic State that nurtured a dharmic living.

The immediate question that may be asked is, 'What is Dharma?' I have covered the meaning and essence of Dharma in the essay 'What is Dharma?' in the introduction of *Mahābhārata Unravelled: Lesser-Known Facets of a Well-Known History*, so I will refrain from repeating the details here. Briefly, the overarching dharmic principle is about sustenance and progress of the society, in fact of any system. The word 'Dharma' itself means 'that which sustains and upholds'. This topic will be covered in parts in this book as well.

A system can only be sustained if all its stakeholders thrive and grow in all dimensions of life—physical, material, emotional, spiritual—in a manner aligned with their innate swabhāvas (natures). A dharmic State, therefore, can be understood as one where the king or the administrator facilitates the establishment and operation of a system that makes it possible for all kinds of individuals, with different swabhāvas and capabilities, to not just survive but grow and thrive physically, materially, emotionally and spiritually, while contributing gainfully to the larger system—community, State, society—of which they are a part.

Dharmic living can be understood as an individual's quest for growth—physical, material, emotional and spiritual—or an individual's pursuit of the चतुर्विधपुरुषार्थ (chaturvidha purushārthas), namely:

- Dharma: Dharma here has to be understood as personal Dharma, in the sense of duty towards self and society as well as religious duties, as prescribed in the scriptures.
- Artha: Material resources, wealth and physical comfort.
- Kāma: Desires, passion, lust, attachments (for and with worldly objects, sensual pleasures, ego and so on).
- Moksha: Eventual, ultimate deliverance from the cycle of birth and death.

Dharmashāstras define the end goal of such a pursuit, which is 'to achieve निश्रेयस—ultimate happiness in this world and the world beyond' and provide theological and practical guidance regarding personal, social and religious conduct of the people that can lead this outcome. Examples of Dharmashāstras would be *Manusmriti*, *Yāgnavalkya Smriti*, *Pārāshara Smriti* and so on. Āchārya Chānakya's *Arthashāstra* can also be included in the category.

Why Is the Mahābhārata Called a Dharmashāstra?

The objective of itihāsa texts in general, and the Mahābhārata in particular, is to give us lessons of Dharma, artha, kāma and moksha for living a fruitful life. I state the definition of itihāsa in most of my talks and I will mention it here once again:

धर्मार्थकाममोक्षाणां उपदेशं समन्वितम् ।
पूर्ववृत्तं कथायुक्तम् इतिहासं प्रचक्षते ।।

A scripture which gives us the lessons of Dharma, artha, kāma and moksha, which is based on events that happened in the past and narrated in the form of a story, is called itihāsa.

Thus, itihāsa is a case study of the dictums of Dharmashāstra. We have seen the real-time interplay of Dharma and Adharma and the consequences emerge very prominently in the Mahābhārata narrated to us by Maharshi Vyāsa, thus, teaching us important lessons for our own lives through the lives of our ancestors.

In addition to the lessons conveyed through the life stories of our ancestors, the Mahābhārata has extensive and detailed discourses on ethics, social interaction, administration, jurisprudence, personal, social and religious duties, and related topics in the form of conversations between people. All these are topics which come under the purview of Dharmashāstra. Hence the Mahābhārata is called a Dharmashāstra.

Rishi Vaishampāyana, Maharshi Vyāsa's disciple, who narrated the Mahābhārata to Janmejaya, categorically states the significance of the Mahābhārata in Ādi Parva, before narrating the itihāsa. He says:

अर्थशास्त्रमिदं पुण्यं धर्मशास्त्रमिदं परम् ।
मोक्षशास्त्रमिदं प्रोक्तं व्यासेनामितबुद्धिना ।।

(This itihāsa of the Mahābhārata) is a treatise of Dharma, artha and moksha, narrated by Vyāsa (who is) of boundless intelligence.

Vaishampāyana further states, 'Hearing and reading of the Mahābhārata bestows immense merit on the listener and reader. Anyone desirous of victory should read this. Anyone hoping to have a child with leadership qualities should listen to this. Study of this history of Kauravas and Pāndavas brings glory, fame, prosperity and heaven.'

He goes on to say:

धर्मे चार्थे च कामे च मोक्षे च भरतर्षभ ।
यदिहास्ति तदन्यत्र यन्नेहास्ति न तत् क्वचित् ।।

(Anything worth knowing about) Dharma, artha, kāma, moksha is found in the Mahābhārata, O King! What we

see in the epic is found elsewhere, too. But what is not in the epic is not to be found anywhere else.

Such is the expanse and the depth of the Mahābhārata!

Is It Safe to Read the Mahābhārata?

There is a superstition in the Bhāratiya society that keeping the Mahābhārata at home and reading it leads to discord in the family.

It is indeed a travesty of common sense that such questions have been raised about a scripture which has been called the Panchama Veda—the fifth Veda—by tradition. Rishi Vaishampāyana's remarks explaining the merits of the scripture and the fact that it is equivalent to a Dharmashāstra should put to rest all such doubts. Let us also not forget that Srimad Bhagavad Geetā, one of the most sacred texts for Hindus, is a part of the Mahābhārata itself.

Harbour no such doubts. Immerse yourself in the study of the Mahābhārata, one of the greatest epics of all time.

What Is the Scope of This Book?

As I mentioned, there are rich and profound discourses in the Mahābhārata beyond the core history of the Kauravas and Pāndavas, which deserve to be widely known.

I did not cover these discourses in the previous book because my objective there was to present the history of the Mahābhārata as revealed to us by Maharshi Vyāsa and debunk prevalent myths around it. I knew I would have to follow up with a second book even while writing *Mahābhārata Unravelled: Lesser-Known Facets of a Well-Known History*, because leaving out these profound sections of wisdom would be unfair to this grand scripture as well as to the readers.

Hence, here I am with this second book, *Mahābhārata Unravelled II: The Dharma Discourses.* In this book, I will cover narrations which are in the form of discourses from Shānti Parva, Anushāsana Parva, Udyoga Parva, Vana Parva, Sabhā Parva and lastly, Swargārohana Parva.

A significant part of Shānti Parva focuses on how a king should govern the kingdom effectively. In that, the grand old Kuru, Bhishma, imparts the invaluable lessons in governance that he learnt from his gurus and from his own experience of running the kingdom of Hastinābpur for many years. Bhishma speaks about almost every aspect of administration including the approach to taxation, punishing offenders (दंड—danda), internal and external security, foreign policy, action to be taken in times of calamity and, most importantly, qualities that make great kings, ministers and officers. Bhishma narrates these guidelines from the perspective of and for the benefit of kings.

While Shānti Parva is the most extensive, discussion of Rāja dharma also occurs in a conversation between Nārada and Yudhishthira immediately after Yudhishthira is crowned the king of Indraprastha. It is a topic touched upon by Vidura too while exhorting Dhritarāshtra to stay on the course of Dharma and prevent the imminent war between the cousins. The entire discourse is famously known as Vidura Niti. Personal development and ethics are also woven into these deep conversations. Two other conversations that I have chosen to include are Vyādha Geetā and Yaksha Prashna because of the profound lessons they have to offer. The sections on Āpada dharma from Shānti Parva and Vyādha Geetā will certainly make the reader pause and think about the very definitions of right and wrong. I have also included a small chapter on an exchange between Krishna and Yudhishthira, called the Kāma Geetā. It is another short but deeply thought invigorating discussion. Yaksha Prashna was covered summarily in the first book. I felt the need to discuss it more elaborately to capture the width of topics covered in the discussion, in this book.

In the end, I have discussed the episode of Swargārohana, the ascent of the Pāndavas to heaven and Yudhishthira's encounter with heaven and hell. I was asked a lot of questions about this episode by readers of my earlier book *Mahābhārata Unravelled: Lesser-Known Facets of a Well-Known History*. Some readers may have a view that this story would have been a better fit in the first book. However, I see this episode more as a discourse on karma and karma phala unravelling eternal wisdom and guidance for dharmic living and therefore more suitable for this book.

What I find astonishing is that the broad constructs in these discourses seem as relevant in this day and age as they were then, thousands of years ago. We may not have kings today, but we do have administrators, policymakers, leaders, institution builders, influencers and ordinary people like most of us. It is true that we are probably more advanced technologically than our ancestors who lived multiple eons ago, but to reiterate what I had mentioned in the introduction to *Mahābhārata Unravelled: Lesser-Known Facets of a Well-Known History*, our innate desires and psychological traits remain the same. Hence, I am sure we will all find wisdom for leading our own lives from these discourses.

Today, there is a widespread acknowledgement of the need to decolonise our minds from Western value systems and philosophical constructs that have limited or, worse, skewed our understanding of our past and present. This has led to a sense of inferiority at an individual level, and suboptimal policies, unsustainable solutions, destruction of family systems and heightened consumerism at the social level. Hence, it has become even more important to understand the 'Indic worldview' of governance and living, one that is aligned with the cultural ethos of our civilisation—a civilisation that has subsisted much longer than any other due to the inherent strength of its philosophy and systems.

The importance of studying and understanding the 'Indic view of governance' cannot be emphasised enough. Not only can such a study throw up interesting insights for solving present-day issues using solutions that could work best for India, that is Bhārat, but it could also help define approaches to solve some of the most critical issues the world is grappling with today, including the widely discussed sustainability problem. One of the key features of the Indic worldview is its emphasis on the alignment of Dharma, artha and kāma. The pursuit of artha and kāma is not looked down upon. But it is important that Dharma forms the foundation of all actions for the sake of happiness and sustainability.

Just to be clear, this is not a call to discard all that is new but to align the new with resilient foundational principles of the past for a better tomorrow. This cannot happen unless we have an unbiased understanding of our foundation.

I would also like to point out to my readers that this book is primarily focused on topics related to Rāja dharma, ethics and personal development. The scope of the discourses as given in the Mahābhārata text is wider, covering topics related to Varna dharma, Āshrama dharma, pāpa and punya, metaphysics of the creation of the universe, spirituality, religious practices, sanyāsa and moksha, darshans and so on. I have chosen not to include these topics in this book. I may discuss them at some time in the future, if Krishna wills.

Some readers will read this book at one go, others may read it a little bit at a time and some others may read parts of it (or even the whole book) several times. Whatever your preference, my hope is that this book will serve as a guidebook and help sprout ideas for dealing with different situations in our lives. My hope is also that this will inspire a sense of reverence amongst the readers towards the astuteness, intelligence, wisdom and far-sightedness of our ancestors, the way it has inspired me.

The discourses and the discussions presented in this book are not in the sequence they appear in the original text. I have clubbed similar questions and summarised answers under specific themes for ease of understanding and smooth flow of thought. In addition, wherever necessary, I have used contemporary framing of words and style while keeping the bhāva intact to make the message more contextual to this day and age. Moreover, depending on the topic, wherever I believed that adding a little colour would help in bringing out the meaning and insights better, I have opted for essay-style writing. The reader will also find text in italics, outline boxes and grey boxes. These have been used to add trivia, explanations and additional information related to the topic being discussed. The explanations are my additions, unless otherwise specified.

The primary reference used for this book is Gitā Press's महाभारत—the edition with Sanskrit text and Hindi translation. As in previous books, to convey the right pronunciation of names while keeping the text simple to read, I have used only the diacritic ā in Sanskrit nouns and names that have an 'aa' (आ) sound. The names ending in 'a' without the diacritic must be read as अ. For example, Arjuna should be read as अर्जुन.

Any errors in the book are unintended and regretted. My sincere request to the readers is to bring them to my notice so that they can be rectified in future reprints.

Before I end, I must express my deep gratitude to all the readers and followers who accepted, appreciated, critiqued, asked questions and spread my work. It is because of all of you that I am encouraged to continue writing. My family and my friends have been my pillars of strength, providing me with their unwavering support and love. I must thank the Bloomsbury team, Nitin Valecha, Sudipto Mukherjee and Sanjiv Sarin, for bringing this book to life, and to Syed Dilshaad Ali for the cover design.

Maa, I can never thank her enough.

श्री कृष्णार्पणमस्तु!

Kartik Pratipadā, Vikram Samvat 2080 Ami Ganatra

Part 1

Bhishma's Discourse from the Deathbed

Yudhishthira's Grief

The unprecedented war between the cousins lasted eighteen days. The war was the result of Duryodhana's insatiable ego, ambition and jealousy towards the Pāndavas, his first cousins, egged on by the ambition of Dhritarāshtra, his blind father. It was fuelled by the unjustified need of his friend Karna to find the validation of his valour in Arjuna's defeat. Duryodhana was supported by a willing coterie of younger brothers and allies patronised by him, and the eventual compliance, even if unwilling, of the elders of Hastināpur, especially Bhishma, Dronāchārya and Kripāchārya.

While the war was between cousins, its premise was more profound. Despite innumerable attempts by Duryodhana and his friends to provoke, the Pāndavas had kept restraint for the sake of peace and protection of the family relationships. But after the extremely outrageous conduct of Duryodhana and Karna during dyutakridā—the game of dice—in Hastināpur, everyone had an inkling that these successors of the great King Bharata were heading towards a bloody confrontation. The confrontation happened when Duryodhana refused to relent even after the Pāndavas had patiently lived through the thirteen years of exile and were willing to settle for only five villages, giving up their claim on Indraprastha. He arrogantly pronounced that he would not give even a tip of a needle's worth of land to his cousins. He proclaimed in clear words that he did not wish to live alongside the Pāndavas. War, then, was the only option left for the Pāndavas.

As is the nature of the war, destruction was unleashed on both sides. The Kauravas and their allies were eliminated, but the Pāndavas didn't have much left to cheer as all their sons and family lay dead on the battlefield. Yudhishthira was shaken to the core and overcome with guilt. He blamed himself for unleashing the destruction upon his cousins and elders. He wanted to renounce the kingdom and leave for the forests. But on persuasion from everyone, including his brothers, mother, Draupadi, Veda Vyāsa and Krishna, he finally agreed to be crowned the king of Hastināpur and help his people and those of other kingdoms to recover, heal and get back on their feet.

The Story of Shālāvrakā Brāhmins and Vyāsa's Advice to Yudhishthira

While persuading Yudhishthira to give up his sorrow for killing his cousins and elders and accept the kingship of Hastināpur, Veda Vyāsa narrated to him the story of 'Devāsura Sangrāma'—the war between Devas and the Asuras—and the punishment given to the Shālāvrakā Brāhmins.

> Long ago, the Asuras and their younger stepbrothers[1] the Devas fought a war for the rulership and wealth of the Deva-loka. After conquering the Asuras and winning back the earth and the Deva-loka, the Devas killed a group of Brāhmins called the Shālāvrakā, notwithstanding their knowledge of the Vedas.

Out of arrogance, these Brāhmins had openly supported the Asuras in their unlawful quest against the Devas and were punished as they should have been.

Thus, those who destroy Dharma and promote Adharma, as well as those who support and facilitate such destruction, deserve to be killed. If a family can be saved by killing one such person or if the nation can be saved by killing one such family, then that action is not considered sinful. Sometimes, Dharma appears like Adharma and Adharma like Dharma. A wise person objectively understands Dharma and Adharma for what they are in the given context.[2]

Encouraging Yudhishthira, Vyāsa said, 'Do not grieve, you have only followed the path on which the Devas had walked before. And if you still wish to grieve, do it through prāyaschitta[3] as is ordained in the scriptures, instead of renunciation. Assuage the pain of those who have lost their kith and kin and crown their rightful heirs, sons or even daughters, as the head of their kingdoms. Also, you should conduct the Ashvamedha Yagna.'[4]

Pulling Yudhishthira out of his grief took a lot of convincing and effort from his elders and gurus. The process of persuasion led to profound discussions and dialogues to which posterity will always remain indebted. These discussions form the biggest of the eighteen chapters of the Mahābhārata, the Shānti Parva and the subsequent, Anushāsana Parva.

ॐ

Meeting Bhishma

Bhishma had arrived in Hastināpur as a young man, well-trained in scriptures as well as in warfare, and an eligible successor to his father Shāntanu's throne. He chose to give up the right to the throne in favour of the future sons of Satyavati. But the ways of destiny are strange. While fate did not allow him the title of a king, the turn of events was such that the entire responsibility of Hastināpur's administration fell upon his shoulders from the time of his father's death until the crowning of Pāndu and the appointment of Vidura as the prime minister. He continued to be involved in administrative affairs even after that. There was no one amongst his contemporaries who could match his wisdom, experience, administrative acumen, skill and strategy in warfare, and knowledge of the scriptures and the laws of the land.

Much against his wishes, Bhishma fought the war of Kurukshetra on Duryodhana's side. He knew that the outcome of the war would be in Yudhishthira's favour, and so did many others, including Dhritarāshtra. But in the war, Bhishma fought like a great warrior should, to the best of his abilities, considering it as a call of duty towards the king of Hastināpur. On the tenth day of the war, he was felled and he lay on a bed of arrows shot at him by Arjuna. Killing him was impossible because death was a slave to him and would arrive only when he desired. It was from this position that he witnessed the defeat of the Kauravas and the victory of the Pāndavas. Even when the efforts to persuade Yudhishthira to accept the rulership of Hastināpur were going on, Bhishma, one of the greatest Kauravas, lay on the bed of arrows in Kurukshetra, waiting for the right time to call his death.

After the war ended, Krishna stayed back in Hastināpur for Yudhishthira's rājyābhisheka (coronation) and to help the Pāndavas settle down. One day, as Krishna sat in a state of deep meditation in his chambers, Yudhishthira came calling. 'What is on your mind Krishna?' he enquired. Still contemplative, Krishna answered, 'The grand old Kaurava, who was a beloved student of the great Parashurāma himself, who is learned in all the Vedas and all kinds of celestial weapons, has been on my mind. Bhishma is one of the wisest people alive today. He holds all knowledge of the past, present and future. Once he leaves his body and passes away, all the knowledge he possesses will be lost to the world. The earth will become lustreless like the night of amāvasya. Hence, Yudhishthira, you must seek his blessings and get answers to all the questions you may have before he embraces death. Ask him about the fourfold purushārthas of Dharma, artha, kāma, moksha, about the Dharma appropriate for the rulers and any other questions you may have.'[5]

Yudhishthira was yearning to meet his Pitāmaha too. Krishna's advice appealed to him. Soon Yudhishthira, along with the other Pāndavas and Krishna, went to Kurukshetra. Sātyaki, Kripāchārya and some others also accompanied them.

The entourage arrived at the place where Bhishma was lying. He was not alone. A group of rishis stood surrounding him. The grand old man was only a dim version of his earlier self and looked like a dwindling flame. The arrows had pierced through his body. They were still stinging him and drawing his blood as he lay on them, unable to move. He was in visible pain and completely exhausted. He lay there waiting for Surya deva to begin Uttarāyana, the movement towards the north. The visiting group was overwhelmed seeing Bhishma in such a state.

While the others stood in silence, Krishna approached Bhishma and asked about his well-being. Praising Bhishma's unequalled willpower, virtues and wisdom, Krishna urged him to instruct Yudhishthira in Rāja dharma. 'Pitāmaha, there is no one who can resolve ethical and moral dilemmas of a seeker like you can. Yudhishthira has been overcome with intense remorse in the aftermath of the war. Through your intellect and words, please help him resolve his mental conflicts and find peace,' he requested.[6]

Bhishma slowly turned his eyes to look at his visitors. He was having difficulty in speaking. The pain was too much for his frail body to bear. 'I am not able to think clearly nor speak clearly. How will I teach anyone anything in this state? These arrows of Arjuna are drawing my blood and my strength,' he smiled helplessly. There was pain in his voice but no tinge of bitterness for anyone.

'With my blessings, you will feel no pain, no sorrow, no fatigue, not even hunger and thirst. All your knowledge and thoughts will flow seamlessly through your speech,' Krishna assured him. By then, the sun was ready to set and the moon had started peeping in the sky. The visitors from Hastināpur took leave, letting Bhishma rest for the night, promising to come back in the morning the next day.[7]

When the sun dawned the next day, Krishna, Pāndavas and the others came to see Bhishma again. Once again, Krishna requested him to share his wisdom and knowledge with Yudhishthira. Bhishma appeared more at ease. His speech was clearer and his energy seemed to have sparked. 'May Yudhishthira, who is himself an epitome of virtue, ask me questions regarding various Dharmas. I will gladly share what I know,' responded Bhishma.

'Yudhishthira is embarrassed and hesitates to approach you. He feels acute anguish for he believes he has presided over the death of his own brethren and elders who deserved his respect. He fears that you may curse him for the destruction caused in the war,' Krishna said, setting the stage for one of the most profound discourses in the Mahābhārata.

To help Yudhishthira overcome his hesitation, Bhishma said, 'Just like it is a teacher's Dharma to teach and engage in austerities, it is a warrior's Dharma to kill his opponents when faced with a war. It is indeed Dharma to kill in a war anyone in the opposing camp, be it a father, grandfather, brother, cousin, teacher or elder—whoever walks on the path of unrighteousness. Those who condone injustice and transgress the order of Dharma out of greed and selfish interests are worthy of being killed by a warrior keen on establishing justice in the society. A warrior who kills thus is undoubtedly righteous.'

Hearing these words of his grandfather, Yudhishthira went closer to Bhishma and held his feet. Bhishma looked at him lovingly and comforted him. He said, 'Son, worry not, I am fine now. Come sit near me and ask me whatever you wish to know.'[8]

Yudhishthira did not waste this golden opportunity. With the humility of a true seeker, he proceeded to ask questions and Bhishma provided all the answers.

Yudhishthira asked Bhishma many questions related to the duties of a king, instruments that help a king reign, qualities to look for in ministers and allies, strategies for success, the origin of kingship, the origin of Nitishāstra—the science of polity, duties of citizens, Āpada dharma—duties in times of calamities, nature of reality, theology and such others. Bhishma answered patiently, using teachings of scriptures, his own experiences of life as well as many anecdotes and stories.

ॐ

Rāja Dharma

Yudhishthira posed his first question, 'The learned consider Rāja dharma, the Dharma for kings and administrators, to be the greatest. Rāja dharma comes with a lot of responsibilities. Like the reins are used to keep the horses in check, Rāja dharma is needed to keep the society in check, it is said. Hence, Pitāmaha, please instruct me in Rāja dharma.'[9]

Bhishma responded, 'Offering my salutations to Dharma, to Krishna and to the learned Brāhmins, I will speak of the facets of this eternal Dharma.'

Bhishma began by giving a holistic overview of the qualities and major duties expected of the kings, some of which are elaborated further in the subsequent chapters of this book. Bhishma explained thus:

> The foremost Dharma of a king is the well-being and happiness of all his people, and the protection of truth and honesty in dealings. It is of utmost importance that he never destroys the wealth of his people and ensures that whatever is promised to the citizens is delivered sincerely and timely.
>
> Only he is fit to be the king who is courageous, truthful, compassionate, composed, has understood the essence of the scriptures,[10] knows how to keep his thoughts and deliberations confidential, has his desires and anger under control and is always engaged in fulfilling the four purushārthas of Dharma, artha, kāma, moksha (that is, works towards holistic well-being—physical, emotional, mental and spiritual—of himself and his citizens).[11]

There is no bigger sin for a king than not providing for the well-being and protection of his people. It is the king's responsibility to look after the welfare of those who cannot provide for themselves.

The king should respect and serve the elders and the learned of his kingdom and make time to engage with them. While engaging with his subjects, he should maintain a happy countenance and speak to them with a smile. He should strive to remain always active and never give in to laziness.[12]

A king desirous of keeping his people happy should behave as ordained by the scriptures and always strive to be industrious, not leaving things to destiny. While success is determined by both effort and luck, luck alone cannot achieve anything without hard work. Luck is, anyway, not determinable; hence I consider industriousness to be the most important. You should not lose heart if something that has been started does not produce the desired result or is met with some difficulties or challenges. The focus should be on making appropriate efforts in whatever task you undertake.[13]

A quote of Shukrāchārya[14] on this is worth sharing, 'Like a snake swallows a rat stuck in a hole, the earth engulfs a Brāhmin who does not travel to learn and teach, and a king who tries to eschew challenges and does not face them head-on. Thus, a king should always remain enterprising, making alliances when necessary and marching for a war against enemies who deserve to be punished, when necessary.'[15]

While a king should never take away wealth from honest people, he should make the dishonest pay. He should proactively keep the anti-social elements in check and periodically make donations to the worthy while also looking after his own material well-being.[16]

A king must take care of his people like a pregnant mother takes care of her unborn baby. A pregnant lady gives up even those things she likes immensely for the well-being of her unborn baby. Likewise, a king should do all that it takes for the well-being of his people, even if it means giving up his own likes and dislikes.[17]

A king who is virtuous, of good character, patient, soft-natured, righteous, with self-restraint, pleasing to look at, and resolute and straightforward in his dealings is never devoid of royal glory and prosperity. However, he must know that although being straightforward and truthful is important, he should be smart enough to keep his thoughts, strengths and weaknesses concealed. He must also remember that a king who is always soft is often disobeyed by his people and one who is always tough tends to agitate the citizens. Hence, he should resort to both softness and toughness as appropriate in any given situation.[18]

There is nothing as potent as truth for a king desirous of success. It is only by way of truthfulness that a king inspires trust in his people.[19] A king who is truthful and righteous is liked by his subjects.

The scriptures talk about six types of fortifications important to secure the king and the kingdom—desert, water, land, forests, mountains and people. Of these, people are the most impregnable and enduring. A wise king, therefore, would govern with compassion towards all his citizens. But being compassionate does not mean being ever-forgiving. An ever-forgiving king is not feared by his people. Such an attitude only encourages unrighteousness.

The school of Brāhaspatya[20] suggests that a king should be like the sun of spring—not blazing hot and not too cold.[21]

There are seven elements that are pivotal to the sustenance and endurance of a kingdom—the king, ministers, treasury, forts, citizens, armed forces and allies. A person who seeks to harm or weaken any of these seven aspects, even if that person is a friend or a guru, must be severely punished. Devaguru Brihaspati enunciates that the king must necessarily punish even a teacher who has lost his sense of discrimination of right and wrong and loyalty towards the kingdom and behaves in a way that is detrimental to the welfare of the kingdom. For example, the great king Sagar punished his own son and exiled him for life for harassing the citizens of the kingdom, and Rishi Uddālaka gave up his only son Shvetaketu for behaving inappropriately with Brāhmins.[22]

The Justice of Rājā Sagar

Sagar was a very revered king of the Ikshvāku dynasty. He was just and kind. He had a son named Asamanjasa. Unlike his father, Asamanjasa was a rascal. He derived sadist pleasure from the woes of others. He regaled in harassing the citizens of Ayodhyā by playing pranks on them which sometimes took dangerous turns. Once, for fun, he pushed the children of some people in the river Sarayu. Tired and troubled, the citizens finally complained to the king. Sagar found their allegations to be true and banished his son from his kingdom for life. Such was Sagar's justice and virtue.

This story is from Vālmiki Rāmāyana.

A king who, along with being extremely patient, truthful and unbiased, does not hesitate in giving appropriate punishment to offenders has no fear of internal revolt.[23]

A king must always strive to keep his treasury full. He must administer justice like Yama and procure and preserve wealth like Kuber.[24]

The learned and pious Brāhmins engaged in austerities, Vedic learning and teaching should always be protected and respected by the king. But if they actively sabotage the kingdom and trouble the people, they must be punished and reined in. This is also affirmed by Shukrāchārya in one of his instructions where he says that a king should imprison and punish even a Brāhmin learned in Vedas if he picks up weapons against the State and comes to fight on a battlefield. Nonetheless, a learned Brāhmin who is proven culpable of any offence should preferably be exiled rather than killed.[25]

It would be a flawed inference if we were to label as discrimination the dictum of not killing an offending Brāhmin for the same crimes where others are given capital punishment. Bhishma does not say they shouldn't be punished; he only says that such offenders should be exiled as far as possible. He also does not hold Yudhishthira culpable for killing Brāhmins like Dronāchārya. He justifies this by saying that it is the duty of the king to punish anyone who revolts against the State or goes astray from the path of Dharma.

The larger context of Bhishma's advice can be understood from Kautilya's injunction on this topic.

In *Arthashāstra*, Kautilya also discourages capital punishment for Brāhmins and suggests they must be exiled, but after proclaiming their sinful deeds and branding the forehead prominently with a mark of their crime—a headless body for murder, a female organ for adultery, a dog for theft and so on.[26] Living a disrespected life with a spoiled reputation is often worse than death.

A king should not blindly trust anyone, not even those close to him.[27] By direct and indirect means, the king must test the loyalty and goodwill of all the people around him.[28]

A king must always be polite in speech but not become over-friendly and make unnecessary small talk with those in his service lest they start taking him for granted and take his orders lightly. Proximity to the king can be misused by people. Hence, a king should always maintain a sense of formality with them so that respect for the king's position is always maintained.[29]

A king should always look out for the chinks in the opponent's armour in times of peace and war. A king who has spies spread out far and wide to collect all kinds of information about the opponents and whose spies can win over the opponent's people and create fissures in their kingdoms is acclaimed by all.[30]

A king should appoint as his ministers and officers those who are courageous, loyal, incorruptible, born in good families, healthy, disciplined, keep good company, possess self-respect while not being disrespectful to others, learned in scriptures as well as traditions, customs and the ways of the people, adept in keeping an eye on the enemies, resolute and honest. The king should ensure these ministers and officers are cared for suitably. And the king must be consistent in his behaviour with them in public and in private.[31]

A king should give up all indulgences and impulsive actions arising out of passion and anger. However, it is not necessary that he should give up such behaviour completely. Sometimes he needs to show anger, take risks and also indulge in pleasurable activities. The key is to give up attachment to them and not become addicted.[32]

Kinds of Indulgences and Addictions

There are eighteen types of indulgences and impulsive actions usually mentioned, ten arising out of kāma (passion) and eight out of krodha (anger). Those arising out of passion are—hunting, gambling, sleeping during the day, reviling others, sexual excesses, intoxication (by drugs), playing or listening to musical instruments, singing or hearing songs, dancing and alcoholism. Those arising out of anger are—backbiting, reckless action, rebelling without a cause, jealousy, resentment, destroying someone's wealth, roughness in speech and giving intense punishment.

Bhishma rightly said that you do not need to shun these outright, especially the passion-driven indulgences. But knowing when to stop and not getting addicted is critical. Otherwise, these become the vices that lead to a person's downfall.

Bhishma then explained the qualities that make a great king.

He is indeed a great king:

- Who is intelligent, aware of the weaknesses of the opponents, understands justice and injustice with respect to the norms of different communities,
- Who is pleasant to look at, shows alacrity in getting things done, has won over his anger and passions, is large-hearted, without rage, active and enterprising and not given to excessive self-praise,
- In whose kingdom, projects that are started also reach their satisfactory completion,
- In whose kingdom, citizens move about without any fear or danger like sons in their father's home,
- Whose citizens have no fear of robbers and antisocial elements, have no need to keep their possessions under wraps (or locks) and whose citizens understand what is lawful and unlawful,
- Whose citizens are engaged and content in their own livelihoods, have self-discipline and control of senses, are charitable, obedient and averse to unwarranted controversies,
- In whose kingdom, people are not given to deceit or jealousy (as their needs and aspirations are duly rewarded through their own work),
- Who is respectful towards the wise and noble persons, understands injunctions of the scriptures and is engaged in generating resources for the welfare of his people,
- Whose ministers, ambassadors and spies know what to do and what not to, and are adept at maintaining confidentiality of their activities and deliberations,

- Who treads on the path laid out by wise and noble persons and works for the greater good rather than narrow personal gains.[33]

Bhishma quoted two shlokas to emphasise the importance of having a benevolent king:[34]

> Shloka from Rishi Bhārgava: 'A man must first find residence in a kingdom with a good king, then acquire wealth and wife. Because if the king is incapable of protecting his life, how will his family or his wealth be safe? For the one who aspires to be the king, there is no other duty as pivotal as protecting and providing for the well-being of his subjects.'
>
> Shloka from Manu: 'Just like we abandon a broken boat when travelling across the sea, these six kinds of people must be forsaken—a teacher who doesn't teach the right lessons, a purohita who doesn't chant the Veda mantras, a king who is incapable of providing protection, a spouse who has a very bitter tongue, a shepherd who wishes to stay in the town and a barber who yearns to live in the forest.'

After giving an overview of the major duties and qualities of the king, Bhishma enumerated the means for effective governance by the king:[35]

> Yudhishthira, all that I have spoken till now is the essence of Rāja dharma. Bhagavāna Shiva, Guru Shukrāchārya, Devaguru Brihaspati, Indra, Manu, Bharadvāja and many others who have propounded treatises on duties of a king consider providing security to the citizens as the single most important Dharma of a king. Let me now tell you how the

king can effectively provide for the protection of his kingdom and citizens.

The king can do this by:

- Establishing a spy network—internally and externally.
- Appointing able ambassadors to represent the interest of the king in other kingdoms.
- Giving timely salaries and benefits to people who work for him.
- Collecting tax from the citizens fairly and smartly but not making the citizens pay exorbitant tax, unjustly.
- Developing in self the qualities of courage, diligence and truthfulness.
- Constantly being focused in thought and action on issues beneficial to the citizens.
- Creating discord in the enemy side using various means and tricks as needed.
- Undertaking maintenance of buildings and temples.
- Looking after the welfare of the underprivileged.
- Using danda (punishment)—physical and material—as a means for establishing justice.
- Increasing the wealth in the treasury.
- Collecting precious items and storing utilitarian articles as may be necessary for the kingdom's smooth functioning.
- Keeping the armed forces motivated through appropriate remunerations and benefits.
- Doing all tasks with enthusiasm.
- Making provisions for the safety and security of the city and citizens; the king should get personally involved in this and not trust anyone blindly on matters related to security.

- Thwarting any rebellion against him from internal dissenters by creating fissures amongst them.
- Keeping a close watch on the actions of allies, those who are neutral as well as enemies.
- Thwarting any attempts by opponents to create discord and instigate people in his service.
- Proactively touring the kingdom to take stock of happenings and security arrangements.
- Not putting faith in anyone fully but behaving in a way that others remain assured and put their trust in the king.
- Upholding Niti dharma—the tenets of ethics and governance.
- Always being active and enterprising.
- Never ignoring or underestimating the enemy.
- Attracting and retaining wise, learned, noble men and women in the kingdom.
- Surrounding himself with intelligent people.
- Keeping uncivilised, dishonest people at bay.

Stressing the importance of a few points in this list, Bhishma continued:

> Incessant enterprise is the foundation of Rāja dharma. On this, Devaguru Brihaspati has made an important observation. He says that it is only through enterprise that Indra acquired amrit, it is only through hard work and efforts that he managed to win over the Asuras and gain control of the heavens. People of action easily establish their domination over people of words. A king, no matter how intelligent, will remain ineffective before his enemies, like a snake without poison, if he has no willingness to work hard.[36]

Never underestimate a seemingly weak enemy while considering yourself more powerful. A small fire has the power to burn down everything to ashes. Only a small amount of poison is enough to kill. Likewise, one with a smaller force but having recourse to a strategically placed fort or a similar advantage can defeat even a mighty army of his opponent.[37]

It is critical for a king to keep matters of strategic importance extremely confidential, especially those dealing with opponents and enemies and those which involve diplomacy and political pragmatism.

To continue to enjoy the trust and confidence of the public, the king should periodically organise and participate in religious activities.[38]

If an officer, a citizen or anyone else, in the interest of the kingdom, informs the king of the malpractices and corruption amongst his ministers which are resulting in the destruction of the treasury or causing harm to the king or the kingdom, it is the king's foremost duty to give such a person special private audience and provide him with adequate protection. This is necessary because it is very likely that the powerful ministers would conspire to get such a whistleblower[39] out of the way to protect themselves.[40]

Managing a kingdom is a huge responsibility. A person who has not achieved control over his mind is incapable of shouldering such a responsibility. Nor is this task appropriate for those who are extremely soft-hearted or very ruthless. All citizens have vested interest in the well-being of the kingdom, therefore being forthright in dealings is always a good strategy. Forthrightness requires a king to be able to behave in a manner which is both soft and extremely tough as the situation demands. To protect the kingdom and

> his people, even if the king must give up his life, it accrues a great deal of virtue for the king.[41]

Bhishma then concluded, 'I have explained to you Rāja dharma and its key components in brief. Ask me if you have any other questions.'

ॐ

Conduct Befitting a King

Having received a comprehensive overview of Rāja dharma, Yudhishthira wished to know about the appropriate conduct for a king wishing to attain happiness and prosperity in this world and beyond.

Bhishma enumerated thirty-six pairs of virtues to his grandson. He said:

> A king who imbibes these thirty-six virtues and puts them into practice attains lasting happiness:
>
> 1. Always conduct yourself in accordance with Dharma without being bitter towards anyone.
> 2. Have compassion towards all and faith in the Almighty.
> 3. Obtain wealth without resorting to cruelty.
> 4. Seek material pleasures which are not against Dharma (as prescribed by the law of the land and social norms).
> 5. Speak that which is pleasing without being mean or pitiable.
> 6. Be courageous but not a braggart.
> 7. Be charitable but do not give charity to the underserving and unworthy.
> 8. Be bold and adventurous but not cruel and ruthless.
> 9. Do not seek alliance with the dishonest and the uncivilised.
> 10. Do not have a war with your kinsmen.
> 11. Do not appoint spies who are not absolutely loyal.
> 12. Accomplish your tasks without causing pain to others.
> 13. Do not disclose your plans and motivations to the unscrupulous.

14. Do not brag about your own qualities.
15. Do not grab the wealth of the honest.
16. Do not give shelter to the dishonest.
17. Do not punish without a thorough investigation.
18. Do not leak your secret deliberations.
19. Do not bestow favours on the greedy.
20. Do not trust anyone who has caused harm earlier.
21. Protect your wives and do not be malicious.
22. Maintain purity but do not hold anyone in disgust.
23. Enjoy the company of women, but not in excess.
24. Eat food that is appetising but is not unhealthy.
25. Venerate the respect-worthy with humility.
26. Serve your gurus guilelessly.[42]
27. Worship the gods with sincerity.
28. Desire for prosperity but not through ways which bring infamy.
29. Partake pleasures without getting attached to them.
30. Be diligent and skilful in your actions and wait for the right time to act.
31. Comfort the needy but not with empty words, just to get them off your back.
32. Do not deride those whom you grant a favour.
33. Do not attack in ignorance.
34. Do not grieve over a slain enemy.
35. Show anger when needed but not without a reason.
36. Be gentle but not towards those who have caused you harm.

'Behaving thus, reign over your kingdom. A king who does not conduct himself as stated here calls for trouble,' concluded Bhishma.[43]

A Procrastinator's Plight

An important quality for a king's success is being active and enterprising. This includes having the ability to foresee the possible outcomes of a situation that is still unfolding, developing sensitivity to a potential threat and showing alacrity in response. To drive home this point, Bhishma narrated to Yudhishthira a parable of the three fish.[44]

> In a pond not too deep, lived three fish who were good friends. One of them was called Anāgatavidhātā[45] because he had good foresight and could predict danger well in advance. The second one was called Pratyutpannamati[46] because he was quick-witted. He had a knack for quickly responding to unfurling situations. The third one was called Deerghasutri[47]. He had a tendency to procrastinate.
>
> One day some fishermen dug out a few outlets from the pond to drain the water and catch the fish. Seeing the water level recede, Anāgatavidhātā sensed danger. He cautioned his two friends about it. 'It seems to me that fish in this pond face a threat to their lives. Hence, while the exit route is still available, we should swim away to other water bodies. One who takes appropriate precaution before a calamity strikes protects himself from trouble,' he said.
>
> 'You are right about being cautious, but I think you are being overly so. There seems no reason for us to act in such haste,' replied Deerghasutri dismissing the tone of alarm in Anāgatavidhātā's voice. Pratyutpannamati agreed with Deerghasutri. He was confident that

when the situation arose, his intelligence would help him to find a way out. Anāgatavidhātā did not argue. He did what he thought was the right course of action and left the pond the next day.

The water drained out quickly and the fishermen, finding the opportunity suitable, cast their net to catch the fish in the pond. Along with others, Deerghasutri, who was lazing around, got caught in the net. Pratyutpannamati quickly assessed the situation and saved himself from getting caught. But he was sure he would not be able to escape the fishermen when they came back again. There was hardly any water left in the pond anyway. So he used his wits and made a plan to escape. He himself held on to the outer edge of the fishing net with his mouth. It appeared as if he too was caught in the net with the others.

The fishermen pulled out the net and took it to the adjacent pond to wash their catch, as Pratyutpannamati had expected. Once the net was lowered into the pond, he acted fast. He opened his mouth to release the net, dropped into the water and quickly swam away. Deerghasutri found no escape. He had fallen prey to his procrastination and laziness. He was caught in the net and eventually died.

'Likewise, Yudhishthira,' said Bhishma, 'the person who, deluded by ignorance, ego or lethargy, fails to open his eyes to imminent danger and take pre-emptive measures before calamity actually strikes, gets destroyed the way Deerghasutri was. Those who, like Pratyutpannamati, considering themselves very smart, do not take precautionary measures in time also lead themselves into trouble but there is a chance that their quick thinking may allow them a safe passage.

But the person who understands the nuances of time, place and situations, always acts well in time after having thoroughly thought through the situation and therefore achieves all that he aims for.'

ॐ

The Need for a King and the Development of Nitishāstra

Yudhishthira then asked Bhishma a question regarding the stature of the king in the society.

'Pitāmaha, what is the origin of the word Rājā? A Rājā physically looks like everyone else. In intelligence and qualities, he is similar to other people. He takes birth like any ordinary person, breathes, feels emotions and eventually dies like any other person. Then what is so special about him that he manages to assert his influence over the society?'

In reply, Bhishma explained how the position and stature of the king came to be and the reason for his dominance, namely a deep understanding of Nitishāstra—the science of polity and governance.[48]

> In the early days of Satyuga, there was no kingdom, no king, no polity, no punishment. There was no need for all that as the people were conscious of their Dharma and lived an honest life, devoid of anger, greed or ego. They needed no oversight as they themselves took care of one another and would not perform any kind of unjust actions. They were happy with what they had and harboured no desire to possess that which belonged to others.
>
> Over time, their intellect started to get muddled. They lost their sense of duty and responsibility. They lost the faculty to discriminate between right and wrong. They were caught in the trap of lust, anger, greed, attachments, jealousy and pride. The society began to fall into depravity and injustice prevailed. The knowledge of the Vedas was lost. Mātsya nyāya

(the law of the jungle—big fish eat small fish) became the norm and people began to suffer. People stopped serving the Devatās and taking care of nature.

Disturbed by such lawlessness, the Devatās approached Brahma deva and asked him to restore order. Brahma deva assured them of finding a solution to the problem. He then commenced to write an all-encompassing treatise on polity, governance, social norms and topics of importance related to Dharma, artha and kāma—three of the four purushārthas needed to establish a just and well-functioning society. He called his treatise, consisting of a hundred thousand chapters, *Trivarga*. Some major components covered in it were:

- Duties and training of a king
- Means of administration
- Importance of the Saptānga—the seven limbs of the kingdom
- Roles of ministers and their appointment
- Internal and external security through spies
- Construction and protection of forts
- Filling and managing the treasury
- Taxation and welfare of citizens
- Stocking and storing of critical items of value
- Generating and investing resources appropriately
- Giving charity or grants to the deserving
- Dispute resolution
- Punishing criminals and offenders
- Promoting trade and businesses
- Identifying allies, enemies and neutrals
- Securing self and country from enemies
- Strategies for dealing with different kinds of enemies

- War strategies
- Protection against various calamities
- Key indulgences and addictions for the king to watch out against and several such issues.

Having created this manual of governance, Brahma deva was very pleased. 'The knowledge in this treatise will help to establish a state of justice and law, of Dharma,' he said. But *Trivarga* was too huge for human beings to absorb, given the length of their lives. Thus, Bhagavāna Shiva, also called Vishālāksha, learnt the *Trivarga* and created an abridged version with ten thousand chapters which came to be known as *Vaishālāksha*. Indra learnt the lesson of polity from Shiva and created a further abridged version called *Bāhudantaka* which had five thousand chapters. Guru Brihaspati shortened it further to three thousand chapters. His version was called *Bārhaspatyama*. Shukrāchārya made it even more concise—to a thousand chapters.

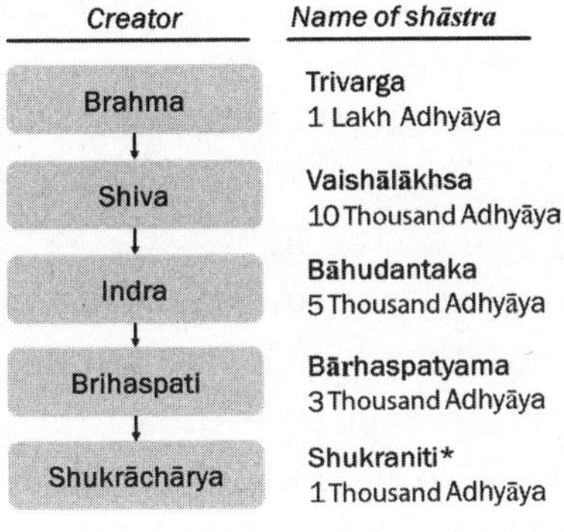

*The name 'Shukraniti' is not explicitly mentioned but it can be inferred based on the work of Shukrāchārya on Nitishāstra, as otherwise known to us.

Evolution of Nitishāstra

There has been a tradition of continuous evolution of Nitishāstra in Bhāratvarsha. This can be seen in Kautilya's *Arthashāstra* as well. *Arthashāstra* is also a treatise on polity and governance to assist a king in making appropriate policies and establishing a system of jurisprudence. In the beginning of *Arthashāstra* itself, Kautilya states that he is not creating anything totally new but building on the works of the experts of Nitishāstra who came before him. He makes many references to schools of Manu, Shukrāchārya, Bharadvāja, Brihaspati, Pishuna and several others. There have been texts such as *Kāmandikiya Nitisāra* written later which use *Arthashāstra* as their reference text.

A point to note is that the focus of the Nitishāstra is the three purushārthas of Dharma, artha, kāma, as these are relevant from the viewpoint of social and interpersonal interactions. Moksha, the fourth purushārtha, is an individual's own pursuits for mukti or liberation and hence it is not a subject covered in these governance-related texts. The subject matter of the Upanishadhic texts is moksha, by and large.

The Devatās were armed with the knowledge of governance but they needed someone who could imbibe that knowledge and use it for governance. They needed a king who could establish a kingdom on the tenets of Dharma and thus protect the people, ensuring they remained honest and had sources of income to allow them to live a happy and just life. They approached Bhagavāna Vishnu with an appeal to find the most worthy person to reign over the kingdom of the humans.

Vishnu gave this deep thought. Then from his radiance emerged his mānasputra[49] Virāja. Virāja, however, was an enlightened being from the beginning itself. He chose renunciation over royal privileges, but not before leaving a successor in the form of his son Keertimāna. Keertimāna too chose the path of moksha, leaving behind his son Kardama. Kardama preferred to engage in intense tapasyā to gain control over all his senses. Finally, Kardama's son Ananga accepted rulership. Trained in the science of governance and polity, he was a good king. His son Atibala was also very erudite in Nitishāstra. He expanded the boundaries of his kingdom significantly.

But power can corrupt. Unless we are watchful, along with power comes ego, delusion and attachment. Atibala became depraved. He was enslaved by his sensual indulgences and was soon destroyed.

Atibala had a son Vena through his wife Sunithā. Vena was ruthless and oppressive and loathed by his subjects. Hence he was killed by the rishis using the power of mantra-infused kusha grass. To prevent the kingdom from falling into anarchy, a king was needed.

The rishis, through the strength of meditation, got a young man to emerge from the right hand of Vena's body. This young man was intelligent, smart, compassionate and was born having imbibed the lessons of Nitishāstra and the Vedas as well as the art of warfare. The young man approached the rishis who had created him, with folded hands, and asked,

'Please instruct me, dear Sirs, how should I serve you?'

'Do that which leads to the establishment of Dharma in the society, giving up your own likes, dislikes, impulses and biases. Develop a sense of equanimity towards all and act without bias as is expected of a king,' the rishis replied. Vainya, the one born of Vena, agreed wholeheartedly. He was coronated as the king and Shukrāchārya became his purohita.

This young man born out of Vena's right hand became renowned as Prithu. Eighth in the lineage of Vishnu, he was the king the Devatās were seeking to govern the society. It is said that before Prithu's birth, the earth was very uneven. Flat lands were few. Prithu, through his efforts, made large areas of the earth even and fit for agriculture. He managed to harness the power of the earth by growing seventeen kinds of grains and other food to nourish his people.

Because he established a state of Dharma—of righteousness and justice—and looked after the well-being of the people and led to their delight, he was called Rājā.

रंजिताश्च प्रजाः सर्वास्तेन राजेति शब्दयते

He is called the Rājā because he brings happiness and delight (रंजति) to his people, through his decisions and actions.

Prithu was also called Kshatriya because he protected his subjects, including Brāhmins, from extinction by providing food and security and reviving the Vedic traditions.

ब्राह्मणानां क्षतत्राणात् ततः क्षत्रिय उच्यते

Because he saved the Vedic Brāhmins (Vedic tradition) from extinction (क्षतत्राणात्), he is called Kshatriya.

The earth is said to get her name 'Prithvi' from Prithu.

प्रथिता धर्मतश्चेयं पृथिवी बहुभिः स्मृता

Because Prithu righteously expanded the earth (प्रथित) and made it fit for civilisation, the earth became known as Prithvi.

Prithu ruled in accordance with the Nitishāstra, keeping his senses under control and being devoted to the welfare of his subjects. Pleased with his tapasyā, Vishnu, it is said, entered Prithu's body, due to which Prithu became venerable to the world as Bhagavāna himself.

The Story of Prithu

The story of Prithu is mentioned in Vishnu Purāna, Brahma Purāna, Harivamsha Parva and some other texts as well. The story in all these texts is largely similar, but his lineage is different in different texts. In Vishnu Purāna and Brahma Purāna, he is considered as a successor of Dhruva and grandson of Manu. In Harivamsha Parva, the lineage is traced to Rishi Atri. In one version, Prithu's father's name is mentioned as Anga instead of Vena.

Therefore, Yudhishthira, seeking the wisdom of Nitishāstra, you should strive to keep your kingdom secure from enemies, and your people safe and nourished.

Two thoughts on the story of Prithu:

1. A king is not venerated because of who he is or his lineage. A king is venerated because he fulfils the numerous expectations from the position he holds—expectations that the person taking the position is required to live up to. One expectation is that he should have a profound knowledge of Nitishāstra and the ability to translate the wisdom contained in it into the governance of the kingdom. Another expectation is that the king should have the disposition to put the interests of his subjects before himself. Such wisdom and disposition can only be displayed by a person who has learnt to subjugate his senses and his mind and has developed keen mental objectivity and emotional equanimity, coupled with a sense of detachment towards worldly objects, especially towards his own ego. A person who manages to live his life with such discipline, shouldering the responsibility of an entire kingdom, deserves respect. Veneration is not for the power he wields but for how he wields the power. Chānakya calls such a king a Rājarshi—a king who is also a rishi.
2. When the Devatās wanted to find the most deserving person who could be the king, they went to Vishnu. Vishnu created Virāja. From Virāja to Prithu was a journey with many misfires. Prithu was the result of all those efforts. It required multiple iterations

to arrive at the desired outcome even in a story of creation ordained by Vishnu himself. A similar theme can be seen in the story of the creation of humans by Brahma deva. In the story, he first created Sanat Kumaras who, like Virāja, took the path of renunciation. It took Brahma a few attempts before he could create Manu and Shatarupā who became the progenitors of the human race.

There is a very important lesson in this—achieving perfection and success is rarely a one-shot process. It requires consistency, hard work, introspection, improvisations and persistence over a sustained period. Success comes to those who keep persevering, with patience.

ॐ

Indriya Nigraha

Yudhishthira's next question was on the duties and responsibilities required of a king and the approach he should adopt to fulfil them.

'What are the key duties that a king should specifically perform? How should he make his kingdom secure? How can he achieve victory over his enemies? How should he appoint spies? How can he inspire trust in all his subjects, his wives, his children and those who work for him?' he asked Bhishma.

The Pitāmaha replied:

> The foremost priority of the king must be to achieve control over his own self. How will he, who has not won over himself, ever win over his enemies? Winning over self means being able to control your mind and the five senses—sight, smell, taste, touch and hearing. Only a jitendriya king, who has won over his senses as well as the impulses arising out of his senses, becomes capable of defeating his enemies.[50]

Bhishma elaborated on the various duties of the king over the course of their dialogue. But the way he chose to begin his answer was testimony to Krishna's trust in his infinite wisdom. Indriya nigraha is the essence of all learning and of Dharma.

Bhishma asserted the importance of indriya nigraha, especially for a king, multiple times during the conversation. To support his assertion, he shared a quote from Manu:

राज्यं तिष्ठति दक्षस्य संगृहीतेन्द्रियस्य च।
आर्तस्य बुद्धिमूलं हि विजयं मनुरब्रवीत् ।।

Manu has said that a king who has controlled his senses (संगृहीत इन्द्रिय) and has competence (दक्ष) enjoys stable reign over a kingdom. It is only through wisdom (बुद्धि) that he can successfully overcome difficult times.[51]

Bhishma further explained the importance of self-restraint when Yudhishthira asked him to pick one foundational virtue that must be practised by all. He said:

> Wise and learned persons have explained multiple approaches to practising Dharma according to their own understanding and wisdom. But all of them concur that the one virtue that Dharma depends on is self-restraint (of the doer). Practising self-restraint enhances the person's तेजस—vital power, and leads to क्रियासिद्धि—success in the tasks undertaken. Such people are happy in every situation. On the other hand, a person who has not achieved control over his senses goes through a lot of grief and pain. All kinds of virtues—honesty, truthfulness, patience, fortitude, perseverance, non-violence, stability, control on anger, generosity and several others—arise from practising self-restraint.[52]

Bhishma stated explicitly that the responsibility of achieving nigraha lay squarely on the shoulders of the individual. Even a king cannot depend on anyone else to make that happen. 'A king can arrive at the right course of action by consulting with others. He can learn about and imbibe appropriate values by studying the scriptures. But it is only by exercising his own wisdom that he can achieve self-restraint,' he said.[53]

The Chariot Analogy

Bhishma's exhortation about control of senses being of utmost importance to a leader is fully supported by Chānakya. Āchārya Chānakya states in *Arthashāstra* that the root of a well-governed and happy State is a king who has achieved control over his senses—राज्यस्य मूलं इन्द्रियजयः. Chānakya goes a step further and states that one of the primary objectives of a prince's education is to train him in controlling his mind and impulses and achieving self-restraint—विद्या विनयहेतुरिन्द्रियजयः.

When a person is not disciplined and is given to sensual indulgences, his focus and energies are scattered. He is prone to responding to a situation from a position of anger, lust, greed, ego, delusion or jealousy, based on merely what gives him pleasure and pain, rather than from a position of wisdom and objectivity. Such a person, enslaved by his senses, rarely responds; he only reacts. Decisions taken in this manner are more likely to cause harm than good.

Response is given after having thought through the situation. Reaction is a reflexive impulse.

The results of incorrect decision-making are extremely serious for a king because he administers justice and shoulders the responsibility of establishing Dharma in the kingdom. His decisions have a far-reaching impact not just on him but on his kingdom and subjects as well. This is the purport of Chānakya's categorical statement that the stability and happiness of a kingdom rests on a king who has achieved self-control.

Kathopanishad has a beautiful analogy about indriya nigraha which deserves mention here.

While explaining the concept to Nachiketa, Yama, the god of Death and Dharma, compares the human body to a chariot (Kathopanishad 1.3.3–1.3.6). He says:

आत्मानँ रथितं विद्धि शरीरँ रथमेव तु ।
बुद्धिं तु सारथिं विद्धि मनः प्रग्रहमेव च ॥

Know the self as the rider in the chariot, body (शरीरम्) as the chariot (रथम्), know intelligence (बुद्धि) as the driver (सारथि), know the mind as the reins (प्रग्रहम्).

इन्द्रियाणि हयानाहुर्विषयाँ स्तेषु गोचरान् ।
आत्मेन्द्रियमनोयुक्तं भोक्तेत्याहुर्मनीषिणः ॥

The senses (इन्द्रियाणि), the wise say, are the horses (हयाः), the objects (विषयाः) which they perceive are the path (गोचराः) the horses desire to take; the self (the ātmā) in association with body, mind and senses is the experiencer (of pleasure and pain).

The charioteer must ensure that the horses stay on the right path, make the correct turns, halt when needed and speed up when needed. For that, the charioteer needs to have the reins completely in his control. Reins left unmanaged would leave the horses directionless, allowing them to run around wherever they felt like, even if the path was not the one that leads to the destination—worse, it might lead to doom. Yama says that the person who has the right faculty of discriminating (yukta buddhi or viveka buddhi) and knows how to control the reins will also be able to steer his senses effectively, like well-steered horses:

यस्तु विज्ञानवान्भवति युक्तेन मनसा सदा ।
तस्येन्द्रियाणि वश्यानि सदश्वा इव सारथेः ।।

Of him who is possessed of discrimination (विज्ञानवान्) and has his mind always controlled (युक्तः मनः), the senses are always controllable as the docile horses of the driver.

यस्त्वविज्ञानवान्भवत्ययुक्तेन मनसा सदा ।
तस्येन्द्रियाण्यवश्यानि दुष्टाश्वा इव सारथेः ।।

But of him who is not possessed of discrimination (अविज्ञानवान्), and whose mind is always uncontrolled (अयुक्तः मनः), the senses are not in control like the vicious horses of the charioteer.

This same analogy of the body being the chariot is made by Vidura in his conversation with Dhritarāshtra.[54]

Krishna goes a step further in Srimad Bhagavad Geetā and says:

वशे हि यस्येन्द्रियाणि तस्य प्रज्ञा प्रतिष्ठिता।।2.61।।
Vashe hi yasyendriyāni tasya prajnā pratisthitā.

Only in a person who has all the sense organs and mind under control does wisdom, that is, intelligence get stabilised.

Now think of the most well-known image of the Mahābhārata which depicts the chariot analogy beautifully—Arjuna on the chariot and Krishna his charioteer!

May Krishna inspire our wisdom!

Statue of Krishna and Arjuna in a chariot at present-day Kurukshetra.

Author

Indriya nigraha is a recurring theme in all our shāstras. Our heroes are those, who have acted responsibly, keeping their impulses and indulgences in check, thinking deeply about the implications of their decisions and actions on the larger society. The anti-heroes are those who have acted only to satisfy their impulses and indulgences, namely greed, lust, anger, ego, jealousy and attachments, without any consideration of society at large, and have eventually gone down the path of destruction.

ॐ

Saptānga, Shādagunya and Trivarga

After underlining the need for a king to control his senses and not give in to indulgence, Bhishma elaborated on the other important duties of a king. While doing so, he laid out three important frameworks of governance—Saptānga, Shādagunya and Trivarga.

> Saptānga deals with seven aspects of great strategic importance for the stability and prosperity of the State. The word 'Saptānga' literally means 'seven limbs' or 'seven assets'. The strength and quality of these seven assets determine the prosperity and sustainability of the State. These are:
>
> - King (स्वामी)
> - Ministers (अमात्य)
> - Treasury (कोश)
> - Army/Security forces (दंड)[55]
> - Allies (मित्र)
> - People and provinces (जनपद)
> - Capital city (पुरम्).[56]

A king should diligently protect these seven limbs.[57]

Bhishma then listed Shādagunya, the six strategies of managing opponents.

> The six strategies of Shādagunya are:[58]
>
> - Making peace (संधि)
> - Frontal attack (विग्रह)
> - Marching for war/Mobilisation of troops (यान)

- Intermediate state of staying quiet and waiting for the right opportunity (आसन)
- Seeking shelter from someone more powerful (संश्रय)
- Dual policy of strengthening self (through alliance and other means) and weakening the enemy (by creating internal discord and feuds in the enemy camp) (द्वैधीभाव).

Managing Saptānga and acting according to Shādagunya could lead to three broad categories of outcomes, called 'Lower Trivarga', for the protagonist State in terms of power and prosperity, in actual terms as well as relative to the opponent. These three outcomes are:

1. Decrease (क्षय)
2. Increase (वृद्धि)
3. Status quo (स्थिति).

The strategy adopted by a king, who wishes to succeed against his opponent, should be aligned with the relative health of the Saptānga of his State in comparison with that of his opponent. The king should act in a way that gives him an advantage over his opponent. This calls for a thorough and unbiased assessment of the strengths and weaknesses of self and the opponent along with building and analysing scenarios of the possible outcomes before any decision to act is taken. The importance of such an assessment cannot be stressed enough.

Bhishma reminded Yudhishthira that all actions of a king must ultimately be geared towards the pursuit of the 'Higher Trivarga', the purushārthas of

Dharma, artha and kāma, for the citizens as well as his own self.

Moksha is an individual pursuit independent of the State. Hence, it is not included here.

'A king who is adept in protecting his Saptānga, assiduously practising Shādagunya, bearing in mind both the lower and higher Trivarga can successfully establish his supremacy over the entire earth,' emphasised Bhishma.[59]

ॐ

Major Duties of a King

Among the many duties of a king that Bhishma spoke of, Yudhishthira had specific questions about some of the most important ones. Bhishma explained them in detail to satisfy Yudhishthira's thirst for knowledge. These major duties can be broadly categorised as:

- Appointment of purohita, ministers, courtiers and attendants
- Appointment of a council of ministers with representation of all communities
- Managing security through the king's forces and spy networks
- Resource generation, treasury management, taxation and public welfare
- Administering justice through danda
- Identifying friends
- Identifying the wicked
- Dealing with adversaries.

For ease of understanding and comprehension, each of these has been elucidated separately.

Appointment of Purohita, Ministers, Courtiers and Attendants

Yudhishthira wanted to know what qualities to look for while appointing ministers, officers and courtiers. 'Because without people to support and help, it is not possible for the king to govern all by himself,' he said.[60]

'Undoubtedly,' agreed Pitāmaha, 'it is not possible for the king to govern a kingdom single-handedly.

Without the help and support of capable people, earning money and generating resources is also not possible.' He described in some detail the traits and characters to look for while appointing people to various positions and roles in the kingdom:

For a Purohita

Have by your side a wise and learned purohita,[61] one who is not given to greed and indulgences and who is adept in giving suitable advice aligned with Dharma. A king who has such a sagely purohita imbibes similar virtues as the purohita, which are then imbibed by the subjects as well.[62]

For Ministers

While appointing ministers, look for the following qualities:

- Noble upbringing
- Virtue
- Sense of discretion
- Understanding of time, place and context
- Understanding of signs, body language and omens
- Born in the same kingdom
- Courage
- Intelligence
- Strong memory
- Implementation skill
- Inherent compassion
- Lack of ego
- Equanimity when praised or criticised
- Honesty and trustworthiness
- Pleasing looks and personality
- Pleasant speech
- Endurance

- Modesty and non-bragging
- Loyalty
- Good conduct.

Along with all these, for a prime minister and people whom the king involves in confidential discussions, these qualities also matter:

- Concern for reputation amongst the subjects
- Understanding of personal and professional boundaries
- Disinclination to hold malice against capable people; rather, respect for capable people and experts
- Inclination to stay firm on the path of Dharma not giving in to lust, fear or greed
- Diligence and erudition
- Resoluteness in keeping his words
- Disinclination to get into unwarranted competition with unworthy opponents
- Sense of gratefulness.[63]

To oversee sources of income generation, such as mines, markets, ports, the king should appoint ministers and officers who are honest and loyal. For tasks related to income generation, never appoint officers who are greedy, ignorant and given to anger. Such officers are likely to harass people through unjustified means.[64]

For Courtiers and Attendants

Appoint as courtiers, those who are modest, disciplined, truthful, honest, capable of effectively analysing and then forming opinions on different topics and situations.[65]

Appoint as your attendants those who are:

- From good families
- Born in the same kingdom
- Intelligent, learned, resolute and loyal.

Do not appoint those who are:

- From families of disrepute
- Greedy, immodest and cruel.

Such people will only serve as long as they have something to gain.[66]

Other General but Important Tips

- Assess the candidate.

Before placing trust in anyone, it is important to thoroughly test the person, especially for their character, expertise, skill and loyalty, amongst other qualities mentioned. This should be for ministerial as well as attendant roles.

- Treat respectfully.

Once appointed, it is important that the king should treat the persons with proper respect and provide them with comforts. Then, giving them full ownership and accountability, he should assign them to tasks considering their expertise and abilities.[67]

Points for Vigilance

- A person of noble upbringing but not well-learned will not be able to make astute decisions regarding topics that require expertise. Likewise, a person well-learned but not of noble upbringing is more likely to lack discretion about what is to be done when faced with certain ethical dilemmas as he would be completely new to them, unlike the former who would have learnt indirectly by seeing his elders navigate such situations.

- A person of learning and intelligence but not resolute and perseverant enough is unlikely to get much done.
- A king should not disclose his decisions to a person who is smart but not loyal or attached to him. It is possible that such a person would take advantage of the king's weaknesses. Moreover, there may be times when the king gets angry and says things thoughtlessly, without meaning them. A person loyal and attached to the king will easily understand and make allowances for the king's moods, but one not loyal is unlikely to understand and might easily get angered.
- A king should be wary of sharing information that demands confidentiality with:
  - A person who is loyal and intelligent but of a crooked mind
  - A person who harbours antipathy against the citizens of the kingdom
  - A person who has close relations with the king's opponents
  - A person who, even though loyal and intelligent, is newly inducted
  - A person who was punished earlier for a trivial offence and then reinstated

Appointment of a Council of Ministers with Representation of All Communities

Yudhishthira followed up with a very important question, 'The qualities you mentioned for the ministers are rarely found in one individual. How then should the king appoint his ministers?'

'You are right,' said Bhishma. 'It is indeed rare to find all the required qualities in one person. I will tell you briefly how you can constitute a council of ministers to serve your purpose.' Bhishma then outlined a potential structure of a council of ministers that could help a king govern the State effectively, having representation from all sections of society.

> In the council, you should have:
> - Four wise and eloquent Brāhmins, well-learned in the scriptures and of virtuous conduct
> - Eight powerful Kshatriyas adept in weaponry and warfare
> - Twenty-one materially wealthy Vaishyas
> - Three Shudras of good conduct, showing humility and adept in their tasks
> - One Suta who is virtuous and learned in the Purānas.
>
> These ministers should be mature, of around fifty years of age, free of malice, conversant in Shrutis and Smritis, humble, unbiased, free of addictions, not greedy and capable of resolving conflicts amongst various parties. The king should hold deliberations with any eight of the trustworthy ministers before taking any decision of strategic importance. Once a decision is thus taken, it should be clearly communicated to the citizens of the State.[68]

Bhishma also gave Yudhishthira a rule of thumb for the decision-making process, irrespective of the size of the council of ministers:

- Seek consultations with at least three trustworthy ministers.

- After giving deep thought to their views and your own deliberation, share the options with the rāja purohita and seek his opinion.
- Share the same with the larger team. If the opinion is acceptable to all, finalise the decision without further vacillations and take appropriate action in a timely manner.[69]

While not explicitly mentioned, it is to be understood that in case of a lack of consensus, the final decision was the king's.

Managing Security through the King's Forces and Spy Networks

Bhishma reiterated multiple times that a king's primary duty was the protection of his people and kingdom. Responding to Yudhishthira's question on how to secure the kingdom, he said:

> The king's security forces should be stationed everywhere in the city, villages, at the borders, in the forts, in and around the palaces and in all locations of strategic importance.
>
> Along with the security forces, the king must also establish an extensive network of spies inside as well as outside the kingdom. The spies should keep an eye on not just strangers and outsiders but also on the king's ministers, friends, relatives and his own children, especially sons. They should be stationed in all important places in the kingdom (of the king as well as the opponent) including markets, gardens, public squares, gymnasiums and places where people gather during festivals and for other occasions. The spies should be asked to

roam amongst groups of ascetics, guilds as well as in community gatherings.

These spies should be recruited after a thorough evaluation and diligence. Important qualities to look for when recruiting spies are:

- Keen intelligence
- Ability to pretend to be deaf, blind, dumb or other kinds of specially-abled persons
- Enormous ability to withstand hunger, thirst, lack of sleep, pain and all kinds of discomforts
- Willingness and ability to work intensely hard

Recruitment and appointment of spies should be a very secretive process. No two spies should know about the other being a spy.

Establishing a spy network is important. It is equally important to break up the enemy's spy network overtly or covertly inside your territory. It is to the king's advantage if he identifies and captures the enemy's spies in time.[70]

Resource Generation, Treasury Management, Taxation and Public Welfare

'In times of peace, how should a king enlarge his treasury?' asked Yudhishthira.

'By focusing on activities that lead to the prosperity of the State and getting the citizens to engage in them, as per the requirements of desha (place) and kāla (time),' explained Bhishma. He described four broad actions for the king to increase the wealth in his treasury:

1. Encourage and facilitate economic activity
2. Levy appropriate taxes

3. Attend to the needs of citizens involved in farming, business, trade and services
4. Impose penalties on activities that drain wealth.

Bhishma suggested:

> A king should cultivate the following qualities that lead to wealth creation—firm resolve, competency, discipline, intelligence, patience, courage and understanding of the requirements of time and place.[71]
>
> The king should ensure everyone in the kingdom has adequate means of livelihood and should discourage begging, except for those on whom the scriptures ordain the task. He should also stop dacoity. Beggars and dacoits deplete the wealth of the citizens.[72]
>
> A king should get more and more of his people to engage in income-generating professions like farming, animal husbandry, trade and so on. He should proactively look after the well-being of the people involved in these professions, acknowledge their hard work and levy appropriate taxes on them. If he mistreats or exploits them by extorting heavy taxes, they are likely to leave the kingdom and settle in other places.[73]
>
> For providing protection and looking after their well-being, a king should collect one-sixth of the income as tax from his subjects.[74]
>
> The way honeybees collect honey from flowers without harming the flower or the plant, the way a lioness gently holds her cubs with her teeth to move them around but doesn't hurt them, a king must levy taxes on the citizens gently, without destroying

their wealth. He must be mindful of the prevailing circumstances of the place, time and people while doing so.[75]

While imposing taxes and duties on the traders and businessmen, the king should take into account their sales, purchases, cost of transportation, cost of labour, profit made as well as the money required for a decent living of the traders. Likewise, for artisans, he should consider earnings from sales, cost of production, condition and type of goods before levying appropriate amount of taxes.

No tax should be levied without considering the income and the effort that has gone into producing it. The tax should not be so exorbitant that it breaks the back of the citizens. No one will work if there are no profits to be made. Therefore, tax should be levied in a manner such that both the State and the people engaged in activities make sufficient gains.[76]

The king must respect and value the wealthy citizens in his kingdom and seek their support in the welfare measures implemented in the kingdom. Such rich people are essential for the well-being of the kingdom and should be taken care of.[77]

The king should behave agreeably towards traders, businessmen and those involved in agriculture and animal husbandry. He should oblige them with subsidies, waivers and such other benefits as may be important and provide a conducive environment for them to live and work in the State. These people are pivotal to the progress and wealth of the State.[78]

Officers who extort unwarranted, heavy taxes from the citizens should be punished.[79]

In addition, it is also important to ensure that the Brāhmins conducting yagnas and those studying and teaching the Vedas are also provided for and are never short of ingredients needed for doing their yagnas. Just like agriculture and trade, conducting rituals as ordained by the scriptures is also important for the prosperity of the kingdom.[80]

Respecting the Wealth Generators

Respecting and taking care of those who create wealth in the society has always been encouraged in the Sanātana Dharma. Let us look at two examples.

In Ayodhyā Kānda, sarga 100, amongst the other lessons of governance, Sri Rāma instructed Bharata the following:

कच्चित्ते दयितास्सर्वे कृषिगोरक्षजीविनः।
वार्तायां संश्रितस्तात लोको हि सुखमेधते।।

Have you ensured the well-being of all people involved in resource generation, including those in farming, animal husbandry and trade? A State's prosperity and happiness depend on them.

In *Arthashāstra*, Chānakya reinforces the message that while taxation is important, a king must protect professions like agriculture from excessive taxation, fines and surcharges, amongst other things (2.1.37). He recommends punishment for a revenue collector who collects lower than planned revenue because it causes a loss to the treasury. But the more interesting part is his recommendation of punishment for collecting more than the planned revenue due to its impact on the people, because it means that the person has extorted more than he should have from the citizens, causing them harm and draining their wealth. The literal translation of his words is 'One who collects twice, consumes the janapada (2.9.15)'.

Bhishma also said:

> For certain offences, such as thefts, fraud, gambling and drunkenness, the king could impose a monetary fine instead of meting out a physical punishment. The money thus collected can be used for the welfare and protection of the kingdom.[81]
>
> There should be strict regulation on drinking places, prostitution, gambling and such activities which lead to indulgence and delinquency amongst the citizens. Because what is a person overcome with passion and desire not capable of doing?[82]
>
> The wealth collected by the king should first and foremost be spent for the protection and welfare of the kingdom. What remains can be utilised for religious activities and for enjoyment. The king should not waste what has been kept in store for future use or contingency.[83]
>
> Plants which provide food should not be cut, neither should fruit-bearing trees and edible roots be destroyed.[84]
>
> Thus, the king should aim to generate wealth through righteous means prescribed by the scriptures and not oppress his subjects by imposing exploitative taxes. That will only lead to the destruction of the

king himself. It is akin to cutting the udder of a cow giving milk and thus losing both the cow and the milk. Only the person who venerates the cow, and takes good care of her nourishment and health, continues to obtain good quality milk regularly. Thus, a king should collect tax while taking care of the well-being of his subjects, like a gardener who diligently tends the garden and in return enjoys its fruits and flowers.[85]

Administering Justice through Danda

'Pitāmaha, according to your definition of Rāja dharma, I infer that danda is of prime importance for establishing order and justice in society. What is the nature of danda? This is what I wish to understand,' requested Yudhishthira.

Bhishma gave an exposition on the approach to wielding danda and said:

> The king who strives to establish order by administering justice with propriety and proclaims apt punishments to offenders is said to be established in Dharma.[86]
>
> In ancient times, Manu propounded that the foremost Dharma of a king was to protect his citizens by using danda effectively and impartially.[87]
>
> Without the provision of danda, the people will destroy one another. Fear of punishment restrains people. Through a proper exercise of danda, the citizens remain engaged in their work and bring prosperity to the king and the kingdom. Therefore, danda is the ultimate refuge.[88]
>
> Scriptures state that a king who doesn't keep the criminals in check has to bear a fourth of the sin

incurred by these offenders. A king enjoys a fourth of the punya earned by his citizens from the good deeds done by them. He also has to share a fourth of their pāpas (sins). Hence, it is in the interests of the king to punish the criminals and offenders and keep their activities in check.[89]

However, while administering justice or in other matters of the State, the king should keep in mind these things:

- He should never discriminate between his children and his subjects. He should treat all his subjects with as much compassion and love as he would treat his children.[90]
- Punishment and penalties are meant to control the wicked, not to fill the treasury of the State. Hence, they should be used judiciously in accordance with Dharma and not based on whims.[91]
- Punishment should be commensurate with the crime. Imposing corporal punishment for trivial crimes should be avoided.[92]
- While resolving disputes between two parties, the king should engage the services of wise magistrates who give both sides a patient hearing and can objectively assess the merits of the case. Fair justice delivery is the foundation of a successful State.[93]
- Never punish any person merely based on the outrage of a group of people or criticism by them, even if the latter are in a majority. Nor should someone be felicitated just because many people are supporting him. Action should be taken only after thorough investigation.[94]
- When faced with a threat of destruction, the king should eliminate the past and repeat offenders who have attempted to harm him or his subjects.[95]

Manu on Danda

Bhishma refers to verses from Rishi Manu in his discourse on danda. Here are the exact verses from *Manusmriti* [8.18–8.19] that he was alluding to. They are from the English translation of *Manusmriti* by Shri Gangānāth Jhā.

पादोऽधर्मस्य कर्तारं पादः साक्षिणं ऋच्छति ।
पादः सभासदः सर्वान् पादो राजानमृच्छति ।।

One quarter of the injustice falls on the person who commits it, one quarter on the witness, one quarter on the members of the court and one quarter on the king.

राजा भवत्यनेनास्तु मुच्यन्ते च सभासदः ।
एनो गच्छति कर्तारं निन्दाऽर्हो यत्र निन्द्यते ।।

Where, however, the person deserving of punishment is punished, there the king becomes sinless, the members of the court become free, and the sin falls upon the perpetrator.

Rāja Danda: The Royal Sceptre

While explaining danda to Yudhishthira, Bhishma also spoke about its physical imagery as the Rāja danda—the royal sceptre or the rod of chastisement. Punishment is embodied in physical terms as a rod that helps maintain law and order on earth. By holding the danda, the king asserts to uphold Dharma in the society.

Explaining the origin of the imagery, Bhishma quoted an incident from ancient times in the form of a dialogue between King Mandhātā and King Vasuhoma.

Mandhātā, like you Yudhishthira, wanted to know more about the rod of chastisement. Vasuhoma obliged and said:

> We've heard that, in the beginning, Brahma deva wielded the danda—the rod of chastisement—to instil order in the world he had created. During a yagna, Brahma deva lost his sceptre, causing anarchy and disorder in the world. Lord Shiva came to rescue and made a sceptre from his own body. He then handed the sceptre to Vishnu for the protection of the world.
>
> Vishnu handed the sceptre to Angirā, who passed it on to Indra and Marichi. Marichi gave it to Bhrigu. Eventually, the sceptre came to Manu to govern the world of humans. Subsequently, Manu passed on the danda to his sons to ensure law and order in their respective kingdoms.

This is how the kings became the wielders of the danda. The kings have to uphold justice and order in the society and usher in peace and happiness for all by effectively using the danda granted to them.[96]

Sengol, Rāja Danda and India's New Parliament

The holding of the royal danda was a common occurrence in Indian royal families in ancient as well as medieval times. The sceptre, which symbolised Dharma, was handed over by the royal purohita to the king at the time of his coronation. The physical danda was meant to remind the king that it was not a matter of entitlement but a call of duty to uphold Dharma, like the great kings who lived before him. It was to remind him that he was carrying a symbol of Shiva himself in the form of a danda and he was expected to live in a way deserving of it.

On the inauguration of the new Parliament building on 28 May 2023, the ritual of the gurus handing over the danda to Prime Minister Modi was performed once again in Bhārat after many years. The 'Sengol' was handed over to Prime Minister Modi by the Adheenams (Shaivite Mathas of Tamil Nadu). It has now been installed in the Lok Sabhā chamber, next to the Speaker's chair in the new Parliament building. The Sengol, with Lord Shiva's Nandi carved on the top, is nothing but the danda that Bhishma spoke of. It was called 'Sengol' in the Chola kingdom and was passed on from one king to another. As we have seen, this was not a new ritual but a revival of Bhārat's age-old custom that can be traced back to the times of the Mahābhārata and probably even before that.

The Sengol that Prime Minister Modi carried was the same one that was handed to Pandit Jawāharlāl Nehru on the eve of India's independence in August 1947 to symbolise the transfer of power from Britain to Bhārat.[97]

Sengol being handed over to Prime Minister Narendra Modi during the inauguration of the new Parliament building.

Identifying Friends

Yudhishthira then wanted to know how to identify friends and ascertain who to keep at arm's length. Bhishma gave a detailed guidance.

There are typically five types of allies:

1. Sahārtha: Friends because of a common cause
2. Bhajamāna: Family friends
3. Sahaja: Natural friends due to kinship
4. Kritrima: Acquired friends due to exigency or pragmatism
5. Dharmātmā: Allies because of the common cause of Dharma.

Of these, Bhajamāna and Sahaja are considered better allies. Caution is recommended with respect to Sahārtha and Kritrima. A dharmātmā aligns only with the king who is virtuous; beyond that, he has no loyalty. But when he believes that a king follows Dharma, he happily gives his support. With such friends, the king must deal smartly and not discuss with them topics or issues not palatable to them, especially because a king desirous of victory has to be pragmatic. According to the demands of the situation, he may have to resort to means that appear just as well as unjust. A dharmātmā is unlikely to understand the need for pragmatism.

The king can consider as his true friend:

- A person who becomes happy with his progress and desires even more success for him and becomes distraught on seeing his decline
- A person who will not survive if he is dead

- A person who seeks to protect him from harm in every situation.

The king should never become careless or negligent with regard to his close friends either. Because one can never be sure of a person's loyalty in all situations. People are known to change their minds often. Those who were considered virtuous are seen to become vile and the vile become virtuous; friends turn into foes and foes into friends. Thus, the king should himself preside over the most important tasks. Putting blind trust in an ally can be both morally and materially dangerous.

But being paranoid all the time of everyone is also not helpful. It is worse than death. The strategy suggested by the masters in this regard is to place trust in a few people who have been adequately tested, at the same time exercising some caution while doing so.

The king should be particularly careful of those who can lay claim to the kingdom (due to the position) and have the potential to generate support and resources to obtain it. Such people are considered as enemies by wise persons. So are those who seek to cause harm to the king in any way.

The king must be extremely careful of his kinsmen, too. Just like princes of other kingdoms, they tend to be envious of the progress of the king and take pleasure in his decline. On the other hand, no one can be happy without his community. It is the community that comes to the king's support when others try to subdue or humiliate him. Hence, it is prudent that the king shows respect and care for his family and community through his words and actions. He should not trust them fully but behave like he does.

Yudhishthira, thus the king who is cautious while dealing with everyone—friends, foes, family and others—sustains his rulership for long.[98]

Identifying the Wicked

Bhishma also shared with Yudhishthira some characteristics of wicked people, basing his advice on a conversation between Indra and Brihaspati. In that conversation, Guru Brihaspati shared some tips about identifying wicked people based on his experience of dealing with different kinds of people. The indications of wickedness according to him are:

- Constant disparagement of others behind their backs
- Jealousy for achievements and qualities of others
- Tendency to turn their back and become silent when someone is praised by others
- Tendency to express disapproval, silent or vocal, when someone is being praised by letting out a sigh, biting lips and shaking their head
- Tendency to belittle people and speak irreverently about them when alone, despite frequent socialisation with them otherwise
- Propensity to promise to a person to do a task but not do it once the person has left, and evade the topic about work completely, when asked by the person again
- Inclination to eat by themselves and find fault in the food offered to them
- Gloating over the sorrows of others and sulking at their joy[99]

- Incessant blowing of their own trumpet
- Inclination to engage in proscribed activities
- Suspicion of everyone and everything all the time
- Extreme meanness and avarice in attitude
- Tendency to disregard a favour done to them, thinking they tricked the person into doing the favour.

Dealing with Adversaries

On Yudhishthira's question of dealing with adversaries and foes, Bhishma shared his deep insights:

> An enemy, be it a child, young or old, can destroy a king who is not cautious. A seemingly feeble enemy can get the support of a more powerful ally at an opportune time and defeat the king. An enemy who holds a bitter grudge will constantly attempt to harm the king's reputation, sabotage his trade and sources of wealth generation and create hindrances in his path of Dharma. Hence, the king who understands the vagaries of time, never underestimates his enemy and never lets his guard down is considered to be a great king.[100]
>
> Through intelligence, the mighty can be defeated, one's own depleting strength can be preserved and a foe raising his head can be restrained. Thus, decisions must be taken after deep thought and analysis and in consultation with intelligent people.[101]
>
> The king must honestly assess his strengths and weaknesses and that of his opponents, as well as the potential for gains and losses, before embarking on any action. After having consulted his intelligent ministers, he must proactively seek conciliation and co-operation with the king who is stronger than him.

He must also ensure that the opponent does not have knowledge of his weakness.[102]

While righteously governing his own kingdom, the king should seek alliance and maintain peace with other kings who possess great qualities and are enterprising, virtuous and honest.[103]

The king should treat with indifference an opponent who is neither helpful nor capable of inflicting any harm on him.[104]

If the king wishes to attack an opponent, he should assess the prevailing conditions before taking a decision. The opponent is fit to be attacked if he is given to indulgences, is embroiled in a war with somebody else, has become weak, is without friends, kinsmen and allies, while he (the king looking to attack) is better placed in terms of strength and capability of the armed forces as well as the availability of resources. Then, after making appropriate arrangements for the protection of his own capital city, the king can order his forces to march against the weak opponent.[105]

The king should not live in complete subjugation of someone more powerful than him. He should strive to weaken the opponent through some clandestine means, such as creating discord among the people close to him and keeping the adversary kingdom on a slow burner by periodically initiating incidents causing harm and discomfort in the subjects through fire, poison or weapons.[106]

A king concerned with the well-being of his kingdom should avoid a straight-out war. As far as possible, he should resort to sāma–dāna–bheda—persuasion, purchase/bribery and creating discord in the enemy camp—to achieve his material objectives. This is advised by Guru Brihaspati as well.[107]

War should be the last resort. This advice is given by Āchārya Chānakya in Arthashāstra as well.

If a much stronger opponent begins to create trouble for the king, provoking him into a war, the king should seek shelter in a fort, make arrangements for security and seek guidance from allies and friends on the strategy ahead—whether to negotiate, manufacture dissent in the enemy camp or fight a war.[108]

And if war indeed is the only way ahead, then the king must make adequate preparations, such as:[109]

- Evacuate people from villages and relocate them to towns or city suburbs; move stables and sheds of animals to main roads.
- Assure the wealthy citizens and the heads of the armed forces and make them take shelter in the forts and places which are difficult to assail by the enemy.
- Move stores of grains from the open country to inside the forts. In case that is not possible, then destroy the stores of grain by setting them on fire, lest they fall into enemy hands.
- Destroy bridges built over rivers for ease of transport and travel and drain the water sources that fall along the path of the enemy's march. If draining is not possible, pollute them to make the water unusable for the enemies.
- Seek refuge with an enemy's enemy who is near your own kingdom and who can challenge the enemy on the battlefield.
- Raze to ground the smaller forts in and around the kingdom which could be utilised by the enemy, uproot the smaller trees and cut the branches of

the larger ones. But chaityas—trees worshipped as sacred—should not be cut.

- Construct large ramparts around the fort with openings on the top to keep a watch outside and attack the approaching enemy. Beyond the ramparts, deep trenches should be built, and iron rods and thorns should be installed in them. These trenches can be filled with water and alligators and big fish can be let loose in them to make it difficult for the enemy to cross over. Make a few openings for ventilation and movement in the ramparts and guard them like the other main doors.
- Instal machinery at the doors for security and mount them with artillery, ready to use against the enemy.
- Get new wells dug and old ones repaired inside the fort for regular availability of water.
- Stock up wood for fuel and make provisions for herbs, medicines and other ingredients to treat those injured on the battlefield. Also store other utilities that would be needed for the citizens' survival, especially if the fort is under siege for long or if there is a prolonged war.
- Widen the roads inside the city for easy movement of people and goods, construct new water resources and set up markets. Some areas should be constructed in the city which can act as hideouts. Storehouses of grains and weapons, residences of key warriors, army stations, stables of horses and elephants, trenches, hideaways and gardens should be set up within the palace.
- Make adequate provisions for all kinds of weapons, artillery, shields and all resources needed to fight the war.

- Get the residences, fields and other areas cleared of inflammable objects such as dry grass and shrubs, and instruct the citizens to light a fire only at night to cook food and avoid lighting a fire except for agnihotra during the summer days, to avoid fire accidents.
- Post trustworthy spies in public places to keep track of the mood and mental state of the citizens.
- Evict beggars, caravans passing through, eunuchs, lunatics, bards and performers from the kingdom. *Spies usually work in enemy territory assuming such avatars.*
- Appoint physicians, surgeons as well as boxers, performers and other people in the fort, after they have been duly tested for loyalty, to keep the citizens healthy and entertained.
- Publicly recognise people who have accomplished daring and difficult tasks for the king with generous gifts, awards and words of praise.
- It is critical that the king never lets his guard down. Any person raising any kind of suspicion or threat should be immediately brought under control. This includes officers, ministers, citizens or even monarchs of neighbouring kingdoms.
- At such a time of threat of war, it is acceptable to disregard the call for help from friends. Protecting your own kingdom should be a priority. The king will be in a position to help friends only if he is secure and has the means to help.

In addition to fortifying his side, the king must also seek to disrupt the enemy side by causing destruction of the fields and grain stores in the enemy's territory and creating dissent amongst his people and his army.[110]

By creating despair in the enemy camp, either by defeating or killing the opponent, the king is cleared of all debts, thus say the scriptures.[111]

Dealing with a Much Stronger Enemy

In response to Yudhishthira's question of how to manage a very powerful enemy, Bhishma narrated the lessons taught by Guru Brihaspati to Indra on the same topic.[112] Guru Brihaspati had said:

> A weaker king wishing to subdue a powerful foe must, first and foremost, control his impulses of anger, fear and excitement that could potentially make the opponent aware of the king's intentions. He should avoid an outright war as far as possible.
>
> While always being vigilant, the king's behaviour should inspire trust even amongst foes. He must be watchful of his speech and speak only what is agreeable to the enemy. He should avoid getting into unnecessary debates and controversies. Like a hunter who, while being extremely vigilant to not alarm his game, imitates his prey's language and then catches it at the opportune moment, the king should slowly, without raising any alarm, bring the enemy under his sway and wait for the opportune time to destroy him.
>
> Even if the enemy insults him, the king should not react. Rather, he should exercise patience and wait for the time when the enemy is in trouble to take any action. Till then he should use spies effectively, to gather information about the enemy's strengths and weaknesses and create dissent amongst the enemy's

people. At the same time, he should bolster his own strengths and gather more allies. But when the right opportunity arises, he should not delay in making the final attack to subdue the enemy. An opportunity lost may not present itself again.

The king should not fight on multiple fronts against multiple enemies at the same time, however strong he may believe he is. Instead, by using the strategies of sāma–dāna–danda–bheda, he should tackle them one at a time.

The Reed, the Tree and the River

Bhishma narrated a story to underline the need to show humility when dealing with a more powerful king. The story is in the form of a conversation between the ocean and the rivers.[114]

One day the mighty ocean enquired of the rivers flowing into him, 'I have seen that when you flood, your strength is such that even the huge trees get uprooted and are carried away by you. However, I do not see you uproot the weak and powerless reed which grows by your banks. Why is it that you spare the reed?'

From amongst the rivers, Gangā ventured to answer. She said, 'The difference is in their attitude which makes us spare the reed and uproot the tree. Even when the momentum of our flow is too powerful for the tree to handle, it continues to stand tall, defiantly challenging our strength. But the reed holds no such ego—it bows down to our power and saves itself, ready to bounce back once our momentum subsides.'

'The reed understands the call of time, place and situation. It knows when to humbly bow down and when to stand tall. Those who adopt such an attitude do not get destroyed even in times of adversity,' Gangā added.

'Thus a king who, after taking an objective stock of the strength and weakness of the enemy and strength and weakness of his own side, behaves pragmatically doesn't get defeated. Wise persons believe that it is prudent to behave agreeably with an enemy who is way more powerful than yourself at a given time,' said Bhishma.

Thus, by taking care of his people, protecting the borders, winning over his enemies and organising various types of punya-accruing yagnas, the king enjoys the rulership of his kingdom, said Pitamaha, concluding the topic of the major duties of the king.[113]

ॐ

Structure of Governance

For efficient administration and justice delivery, Bhishma described a hierarchical structure of devolution of responsibilities dividing regions into smaller units of governance.[115] According to that, there was:

- One head for every village
- One chief for a group of ten villages or village heads
- One officer for every two such chiefs of ten villages, that is, one officer for twenty villages
- One senior officer for five such officers, that is, one senior officer for hundred villages
- One higher officer for ten such senior officers, that is, one higher officer for thousand villages
- And so on, depending on the size of the kingdom.

The responsibilities of the village head were:

- Keep track of the people and the happenings in the village.
- Investigate local crimes and resolve disputes.
- Collect tax revenue and fines from the villagers according to the policies made by the king.
- Make arrangements for the security and the protection of the village.
- Provide regular updates on all these to the chief of ten villages.

The chief of ten villages was responsible for compiling all information received from the village heads under his control and relaying it to the officer above him, who in turn would send it to the officer above him. Eventually, the senior-most officer would compile all the necessary information about the villages in the kingdom and provide a regular update to the king.

The responsibility of jurisdiction and governance of the villages was with the higher officer in charge of thousand villages. Likewise, every city would also have a city superintendent to oversee the day-to-day functioning and administration of the city.

An honest minister would oversee the functioning of these higher officers and superintendents. Through spies, the king and the minister would keep an eye on the activities and intentions of the officers and ensure the citizens were protected from persons of wicked disposition and deeds.

ॐ

Rules of War

Yudhishthira then enquired about the rules of war. He asked, 'If one king attacks another, how should the attacked king fight back?'

In response, Bhishma narrated the rules of warfare:[116]

- A single warrior should challenge another single warrior for a fight.
- A warrior not wearing armour on the battlefield should not be attacked.
- But a challenge by a solitary warrior wearing armour should be accepted. The warrior should accept the challenge and gear up to fight, wearing armour himself.
- A challenge by an army should be faced by the army. The king should get his army ready to counter such a challenge.
- In a war, deceit should be responded with deceit and righteousness with righteousness.
- An opponent in trouble or frightened or defeated should not be attacked.
- A chariot warrior should challenge only a chariot warrior. A warrior on horseback should not challenge a chariot warrior.
- Warriors should not use poisoned or barbed arrows in a battle. These are the weapons of the wicked.
- A warrior who is childless or has become unconscious[117] should not be attacked. Neither should a warrior whose weapons are broken or is in some kind of distress or whose vehicle (ride) is destroyed or whose bowstring is broken.

- If a severely injured opponent is found, he must either be sent to his home or treated for the wounds. Once healed, he should be freed. This is indeed the tenet of Sanātana Dharma.
- An opponent whose armour is destroyed, who surrenders folding his hands and dropping his weapons on being captured, should not be killed.
- Only a king or a prince should fight another king or a prince in a battle.
- If a Brāhmin or someone not fighting in the battle comes on the field to get the two sides to negotiate, then both sides should refrain from fighting at that time to respect the negotiator. Under no circumstance should such a person be killed on the battlefield.

The Karna–Arjuna Combat That Was Not to Be

The homecoming of princes of Hastināpur, the Kauravas and the Pāndavas, having completed their education with Dronāchārya, was being celebrated with a demonstration of the various skills they had acquired in the gurukula. When the princes were demonstrating their skills, a young man came and insisted on demonstrating his skills in archery as well. He asserted that he was better than Arjuna. This person was Karna.

Karna was a student of Dronāchārya, but he quit the gurukula to find another guru who would teach him Brahmāstra, as Drona had refused to do so.

As Karna was known to Dronāchārya and others, he was allowed to show his skills. But Karna wasn't satisfied with just that. He challenged Arjuna to a duel. Everyone, including Drona, Kripa and Bhishma, was shocked at this. Not the one to back out, Arjuna accepted the challenge. Karna's actions were completely uncalled for. This was not a battleground of warriors but a happy occasion to mark the return of the princes. The unwarranted confrontation couldn't be allowed.

Kripāchārya applied his wit and saved the situation. He quoted the 'rules of war' (along the lines of Bhishma's answer to Yudhishthira). 'Only a king or a prince can challenge a king or a prince, or a Kshatriya can challenge another Kshatriya,' he said.

Karna was not a prince nor a Kshatriya. He was a Suta (through his foster parents), a mixed jāti, an offspring of a Brāhmin mother and a Kshatriya father. Duryodhana knew Karna and his hatred for Arjuna since their days in gurukula and was thrilled to see him. He crowned Karna as the king of Anga, the home state of Adhiratha, Karna's father and Dhritarāshtra's close friend. No one present there objected to the coronation. By then, the sun had set, and the unnecessary fight was averted, thanks to the presence of mind of Kripāchārya.

At a superficial level, this 'rule' is seen as discriminatory. Such an inference trivialises the purpose of this rule and the wisdom of the rishis. If the idea was 'discrimination', then someone or the other would have objected to the crowning of Karna. Itihāsa has a mention of many warriors from the Suta community, including some as powerful as Keechaka, as well as the brothers and sons of Karna himself. They fought wars and ruled kingdoms too.

This rule has to be seen in the context of limiting the power of the king and the other Kshatriyas who learnt the art of warfare in the normal course. But others may not have had the same opportunity. In the absence of such a rule, a prince or a Kshatriya may go around challenging anyone they wished to trouble and the other person, even if not skilled in warfare, would have no recourse. The rule is meant to prevent overreach by those who have power and to protect ordinary citizens. Karna's desire was a reflection of his misplaced judgement and huge ego that was, very correctly, not entertained.

Bhishma also gave some advice to Yudhishthira on how a victorious king should behave after having won over his adversary.[118] He said:

- The king should not attack an opponent who has already been overpowered by force. Instead, the opponent should be captured and schooled for a year in the king's palace. After that, if he agrees to the king's suzerainty, he should be released.
- Similarly, if a maiden is brought home with the intention to marry her by show of valour,[119] the victorious king should allow the lady to make up her mind and wait for her decision for a year without resorting to force. After a year, if she chooses not to wed the king and seeks release, she should be allowed to go.
- The victorious king should never use the wealth obtained from criminals, offenders and opponents for himself, but use it for social causes.

- If the vanquished opponent seeks forgiveness, his wealth should be returned to him.
- A victorious king should calm down the citizens of the kingdom he has won by way of sweet and comforting speech and conferring material gifts. If the citizens are treated with unwarranted ruthlessness, they are likely to espouse enmity against the victorious king, ally with other kings and wait for the opportune time to strike back and seek revenge.
- The victorious king should not destroy the people and the property of the defeated to such an extent that they become desperate and lose their desire to live.
- The righteous should aim to win over the unrighteous through rightful means only. It is better to die than resort to unrighteousness. No king who claims victory, even if it is over the entire earth, through unrighteous means is ever respected.

'A king should desire victory and glory but not by deceit and treachery. Instead, he should strive for eminence by achieving expertise in all kinds of sciences and skills,' stressed Bhishma.[120]

ॐ

Duties of the Citizens

'Pitāmaha, what is the most important duty of the citizens of the kingdom?' asked Yudhishthira.

Bhishma replied:

> Coronating an able king to protect and govern the kingdom is one of the most important duties of the citizens. Without an able king, the country will fall into anarchy and there will be no justice, no Dharma, no law and order in the country. People will then destroy one another and eventually the society. Just as a big fish eats a small fish in the ocean, the bully will have his way in the kingdom by harassing the weak. Such a kingdom will become vulnerable to dacoits as well as enemy attacks.
>
> Hence, it is necessary for the citizens to ensure they choose a king who can govern them justly, establishing the rule of Dharma. Once they have identified such a king, they must obey him, respect him and support him by paying taxes and offering him appropriate gifts occasionally. They should stand by him and support him in every way when he is faced with challenges.
>
> If a very capable and powerful king attacks a State which is in anarchy, the citizens must wholeheartedly accept the attacker king as their ruler. The king may be kind to them if they do not resist.[121]

When Is a Nation Dead?

In the Yaksha Prashna episode that occurred when the Pāndavas were in vanvās, one question that Yaksha poses to Yudhishthira was—कथं राष्ट्र मृतं भवेत्?

When is a nation considered dead? To this, Yudhishthira answered—मृतं राष्ट्रमराजकम्। *A nation in a state of anarchy is as good as dead.*

Bhishma states that ensuring that anarchy does not prevail is not just the responsibility of the king but also of the citizens.

ॐ

Understanding Satya and Dharma

Yudhishthira then asked a very foundational question, 'Truth and untruth both engulf the world. Then how does the one who wishes to remain steadfast in Dharma differentiate truth from untruth? How can he understand Dharma? When is it appropriate to speak the truth and when should one rather not?'

Bhishma replied:

> Truth is paramount. There is nothing greater than truth. But understanding the real nature of truth can be difficult. Let me explain.
>
> Sometimes what appears to be the truth does more harm than good and what appears to be an untruth turns out to be benign. In such a situation, the apparent falsehood is indeed the truth and the apparent truth is akin to untruth. This is also the case with Dharma. Then how can we make sense of truth and of Dharma?
>
> Some say that Dharma is only that which the Shrutis (Vedas) expound. Not so, say some others. I wish not to criticise either side. But then, not everything is covered in the Shrutis.
>
> If some people, with the intention of stealing someone else's wealth, make enquiries about it, then, on being aware of their intention, not telling them the truth is undoubtedly Dharma. If, in such a situation, it is possible to escape without having to say anything, then the person must do so. But if remaining silent is not an option and is likely to raise more suspicion, then it is better to lie than to tell the truth. If a person can escape wicked people by taking

a false oath, the person must do that, but under no circumstance should wealth be allowed to go into their hands. Wealth given to such wicked and sinful people will cause trouble, even for the giver.

Similarly, when someone's life is at stake, or if one is at risk of losing everything he has or on the occasion of marriage, or for the sake of protection of one's wealth, life and virtue, telling the untruth incurs no sin.

Dharma, therefore is that which leads to sustainability, prosperity and well-being of the society. That which doesn't cannot be Dharma.

प्रभवार्थाय भूतानां धर्मप्रवचनं कृतम्।
यः स्यात्प्रभवसंयुक्तः स धर्म इति निश्चयः।।

Dharma has been explained for the well-being and prosperity of society. Hence only that which leads to the well-being and prosperity of society can be Dharma.

धारणाद्धर्ममित्याहुर्धर्मेण विधृताः प्रजाः।
यः स्याद्धारणसंयुक्तः स धर्म इति निश्चः।।

Because it upholds it is called Dharma. Only through Dharma is the society sustained. Hence, only that which leads to the sustainability of the society can be Dharma.

However, those who leave the path of truth for their own convenience and seek the path of unrighteousness and deceit for fulfilling their indulgences must most definitely be punished, even slain. Such persons do not think twice about committing a crime or harming others to get what they want. Society should not

> tolerate such criminals. Slaying the unrighteous who belittle Dharma incurs no sin. They are already killed by their own actions and the one who punishes them invites no kārmic repercussions.

Summing it up for Yudhishthira, Bhishma gave a practical suggestion on practising Dharma:

> A person should be served in the same coin as he serves others. Deceitful should be responded with deceit and honest ones with honesty.[122]

यस्मिन्यथा वर्तते यो मनुष्यस्तस्मिंस्तथा वर्तितव्यं स धर्मः ।
मायाचारो मायया वर्तितव्यः; साध्वाचारः साधुना प्रत्युदेयः ।।

Dharma and Satya

Arjuna grappled with a similar dilemma on the seventeenth day of the Kurukshetra war when he and Yudhishthira had a verbal tiff. Arjuna was faced with two options—to fulfil his vow and kill his elder brother or break his vow. That is when Krishna explained the nuances and context-specific nature of Dharma and Satya and how important it was to develop viveka buddhi—a sense of discretion—to understand what action is aligned with Dharma when faced with such Dharma sankatas (ethical dilemmas). This incident appears in Karna Parva.[123]

This event and Krishna's subsequent explanation to Arjuna have been covered in detail in the chapter 'The Friendship That Groomed' in the earlier book *Mahābhārata Unravelled: Lesser-Known Facets of a Well-Known History*.

ॐ

Rāja Dharma and the Peacock Analogy

Bhishma had explained various aspects of administration in great detail in response to questions posed by Yudhishthira. It was a lot of information to digest in one go. Hence, Yudhishthira requested Bhishma to summarise Rāja dharma once again.[124] Bhishma repeated some of the tenets of Rāja dharma for his grandson's benefit. This time, though, he explained the concept giving an analogy of a peacock to elucidate his points.

> Like the snake-eating peacock adorns himself with feathers of many hues, the king should display the various hues of his personality befitting a king in accordance with the requirement of the time and place. He must be strict if needed, or display crookedness if the situation demands it. He should exhibit fearlessness, truthfulness, sincerity and, at the same time, maintain a sense of enigma if it would serve his purpose—all the while remaining impartial, neutral and righteous mentally. Behaving thus, he can ensure success in the subtlest task without faltering.
>
> Just like a peacock goes completely silent in autumn, the king should fiercely protect his confidential counsel, staying silent and disclosing nothing, not by words nor by body language. In general, the king should be very mindful and restrained in speech and speak only what is agreeable.
>
> The king should be as ruthless with his enemies as a peacock is with snakes, leaving none to even exist in his vicinity. The king should surround himself with virtuous and trustworthy allies.

> Like a peacock who is admired when it opens its beautiful feathers, the king should indulge in and showcase tasks which are respected and admired by the people.
>
> Like a peacock gleans insects carefully even from dense thickets, the king should gather wisdom from everyone and everywhere.
>
> Behaving thus, a wise king must govern his kingdom and adopt policies beneficial to him and his prajā.[125]

Concluding with a summary of Rāja dharma, Bhishma said:

> Through conciliatory words, a king should inspire trust in others. He must have the wisdom and eloquence to engage others in what must be done and discourage them from what must not be done. He must not flinch from display of power, when necessary. And he must make decisions only after having given them thorough consideration using his own intelligence.[126]
>
> A king should do what brings joy to his citizens, but in a way that is not opposed to Dharma. The king who is considered by the citizens as their own, whose anger and joy both have a purpose and are unfailing in their results, who personally supervises important tasks related to governance and keeps track of his treasury with his own eyes enjoys steady rulership and prosperity.[127]
>
> A prosperous kingdom, which has an abundance of food and wealth, whose citizens are patriots and committed to the king, whose ministers are content, is considered to have a strong foundation.

> A kingdom where the purohitas and teachers are well-learned in scriptures and they, as well as other learned and venerable people, are treated with respect by the king is said to be wise.

'I have narrated to you, in brief, the Rāja dharma as ordained by the scriptures. A king who governs after having imbibed this wisdom acquires lasting rulership of this earth. However, a person who acquires his kingdom immorally or by a stroke of luck or violence but believes it to be his rightful possession lacks the understanding of Rāja dharma and doesn't last long.[128]'
Thus, Bhishma generously shared all his knowledge and wisdom for the benefit of Yudhishthira and also for the benefit of all of us.

ॐ

Āpada Dharma: The Dharma in Times of Distress

Yudhishthira then raised a very pertinent question. 'In a situation when all the conditions are against a king—he has lost his allies, his enemies have overpowered him, his treasury has depleted, his army has dwindled, he is surrounded by wicked ministers and he is at the risk of being dethroned by internal or external forces—what is the suitable course of conduct for him? Is it to give up his life or gather wealth by hook or by crook in order to stay alive?'

Bhishma smiled and said:

> You have asked me a very profound question. I wouldn't have broached this topic myself but now that you have, I will answer your question.
>
> Dharma is extremely subtle and nuanced. It is only through imbibing the wisdom of the scriptures that a person can begin to understand it. Rare are the people who learn the scriptures and then actually live the virtues contained there in their lives. I will now tell you about Upāya dharma (उपायधर्म), an approach to adopt in distress, which has great merit. However, strictly speaking, from the point of view of morality, I wouldn't call such an approach righteous.[129]
>
> What can be expected from a person in ordinary circumstances is different from what can be expected when that person is in utter distress. In distress, the utmost priority is to get out of the adversity. In such situations, actions which are otherwise discouraged become acceptable. Concessions are made regarding eating norms, suitability of professions to engage

in as well as performing activities which would be regarded with contempt in ordinary times. This is because the need for survival is paramount in these situations.

If the king has lost all his wealth and is at risk of losing his kingdom to his enemies, he should explore all possible options for obtaining resources to stay afloat, like a thirsty person looking for water. The options include collecting extra money from his citizens so that he is able to protect them from enemies.

A king's strength rests on his military prowess and treasury. A weak king with an empty treasury is not respected even by his own citizens. A king with power and wealth is honoured. Wealth even manages to conceal some of the flaws of the king.

The backbone of a full treasury is the king's military. How can a weak king have a treasury and how can one without treasury have strength? How can a weak king have a kingdom and without a kingdom how can he achieve prosperity? The well-being of the citizens depends on the prevalence of Dharma. The maintenance of Dharma requires the State to have both monetary as well as military prowess.

A rich state with weak defence will be easily attacked and robbed of its wealth by enemies. Hence, to ensure the wealth stays, having a strong and well-functioning military is crucial. That is the purport of the statements above.

Collecting wealth for the treasury is difficult without inflicting some pain. But wealth should not be accumulated by employing extremely cruel means. In times of distress, the approach should be to adopt a middle path. The king who inflicts some pain on the citizens to raise money for sustaining the military

> in adverse circumstances incurs no sin. Following the norms of what is proper during normal times in adverse times is incorrect if it aggravates distress.
>
> However, imposing this burden on citizens should not become a norm or a tool to exploit them. Once the situation turns around and settles down, the king should use the acquired and unspent wealth for the welfare of the citizens. The premise here is that both the king and the citizens should protect each other by every possible means in times of distress.
>
> There is no bigger Dharma for a king than protecting his kingdom at all costs. Therefore, whatever has been mentioned as Upāya dharma is for a king and only in adversity, not otherwise.[130]

Bhishma also categorically mentioned that as far as possible, in perverse times, the king should seek to extract additional wealth primarily from the delinquent citizens and enemies of the State, those who are heretics or given to indulgences and unfair dealings, rather than those who engage in pious and honest activities.[131]

Yudhishthira continued the same line of questioning and posed another adverse scenario. 'Suppose a king becomes weak due to his own negligence and his wealth has depleted, his friends have deserted him, his ministers are divided or have been bought out by the enemies, his army has dwindled, and he is also troubled by powerful enemies. In such a hopeless situation, what should he do?' he asked.

Bhishma replied, 'The king should make peace with the enemy without wasting any time if he is known to be righteous and eventually convince him to return lost territory. If the enemy is cruel but powerful, it is still advisable to make peace with him even at the cost of losing some territory. If the enemy is not willing to make peace, the king incapable of fighting should escape from his capital and save his life. Only if he stays alive will there be any opportunity to come back stronger and capture what he has lost.'

'If the enemy has already laid siege to the king's fort and is creating trouble for the kingdom, the king's ministers are angry with him, and his confidential discussions are divulged to the enemies, what should the king do then?' asked Yudhishthira.

Bhishma answered, 'In that case, as I said earlier, if the opponent is known to be righteous, the king should try to make peace with him. But if the opponent is unrighteous, the king should not give in and rather confront him bravely. Even though small, if the army is committed, the king, displaying valour, can still win the battle. If he dies on the battlefield, he will attain heaven and if he wins, he will gain the respect of his citizens and get to enjoy his kingdom.'[132]

Yudhishthira had another question, 'What if multiple enemies attack the king, seeing him in trouble? How should he decide who to ally with and who to continue to have a war with? No one but you, Pitāmaha, can give me a sound answer to deal with such a situation.'

Bhishma narrated a parable of the sharp-witted mouse to explain the potential strategy to adopt in a situation where a king, already troubled by one enemy, is attacked by others, too, taking advantage of his vulnerabilities.[133]

> Once upon a time, in a forest stood a huge banyan tree providing shelter to numerous birds and animals. At its foot there was a hole in which a mouse named Palit lived. A large cat named Lomesh would come every night to find shelter on one of the tree's branches. The forest was often frequented by a hunter who came and spread his net in the evenings and the next morning carried away the unfortunate animals who got caught in it.
>
> One evening, the hunter came as usual, spread his net and went away. Unfortunately, the cat was roaming around carelessly and got caught in the net. Palit saw Lomesh entangled in the net, struggling to break free. He was pleased to see his enemy in trouble. Until then, Palit would avoid coming out of his hole when Lomesh was around. He used to live in constant fear of becoming the cat's dinner. But with Lomesh caught, Palit had no fear. He came out of his hole and frolicked around. 'Oh, how stupid must this cat be to get caught in a net like this,' he thought to himself and smiled, enjoying his new-found freedom.
>
> But his joy didn't last too long. When Palit was scrounging around for some food to eat, he saw a piece of flesh in the hunter's net. Having no fear of the cat, he climbed up on the outer side of the net to nibble on the flesh. Suddenly, he sensed some movement behind him. He turned around to find two intense copper-red eyes staring at him hungrily. A mongoose named Harin had smelled the presence of the mouse in the vicinity and had come looking

for a feast. At that very moment, Palit heard an eager hoot of an owl. He looked up to find the owl looking at him piercingly, ready to gobble him up any moment.

Palit shuddered in fear. He couldn't run down from the net as the mongoose would catch him in no time. And if he kept sitting on the net, the owl would swoop down and carry him off in his beak. The only option Palit had was to hide inside the net, but that wasn't too smart either as Lomesh would eat him up. The cat was already unhappy about being caught and very hungry.

Palit could see death staring at him, but he was not the one to give up easily. 'No doubt adversity has befallen me, but I must do my best to save my life. I take pride in my smartness and today I must put it to use and seek a way out of this life-threatening situation. I should think of negotiating with one of these enemies. I can offer one of them help with something that they consider very crucial and get protection for my life in return. Wise beings have said that when in distress, one should even befriend one's enemies if it helps them survive,' he thought.

At that point, the only other creature facing adversity in equal measure was Lomesh. Palit knew he had one strength which he could use to save himself—his ability to gnaw through the net in which Lomesh was trapped. He could offer to set Lomesh free from the hunter's net and seek his protection from the mongoose and the owl in return. It could be a win-win situation for both.

Palit spoke to Lomesh and shared his idea with him. 'Brother, it is said that by walking seven steps together people become friends. You and I have lived together happily in this jungle, you on the branch of this banyan and I at its base, for years. By that, you are indeed my dear friend. Today both our lives are in danger. But if you promise to give up the desire to kill and eat me, I have a plan which will save your life. You cannot escape the net without my help. I too will be dead soon enough if I don't get your protection,' he told Lomesh.

Lomesh was already desperate. He was willing to align with anyone who would set him free. He agreed promptly and promised to do all he could to repay Palit's favour. He asked Palit the strategy he intended to follow. 'I will come inside the net. You hold me in your lap. Seeing us together, the mongoose and the owl will give up on me and leave. Once they leave, I will gnaw through the net and set you free,' Palit replied.

Lomesh was excited at the possibility of finally becoming free and asked Palit to come in. 'Have no fear of me any more, dear friend. I will remain indebted to you forever if you liberate me from this net. Come in right away,' he said.

The mouse quickly slipped inside and lay over the cat's chest, looking relaxed. As Palit had expected, both the mongoose and the owl walked away disappointed. The danger hovering over Palit's life was now averted. To keep his side of the deal, Palit began gnawing at the net, but taking his own sweet time. Lomesh began to get restless. 'Why don't you hurry up and get the job done? You can surely cut the net faster than this,' he said.

But still, Palit showed no haste. 'Be patient my friend and trust me when I say that I will set you free at the right time. Work that is done when the time is not right either gets derailed or results in unfavourable outcomes. While we have agreed to befriend each other to achieve our common goal, how can I forget that our species are natural enemies? You are way more powerful physically. If I set you free now, it is possible that your feelings towards me may change and you may kill me to satisfy your hunger. I am your food, after all. However, if I free you just before the hunter arrives, your concern will be to save yourself from him rather than going after me. That will allow me time to escape to safety from you.'

Lomesh was irritated but he knew his life depended on the mouse. He said, 'Do you think I will be that ungrateful that I will attack the one who saved my life? I kept my side of the deal trusting you fully and now I expect you to reciprocate. Rest assured I will not harm you. I apologise to you for my past actions that may have caused you pain.'

'Neither friends nor enemies are permanent. Friends can become foes and foes can turn into friends when the situation demands. Everyone is wired to seek their own interest. Even relationships are based on alignment of mutual interest. Hence, the wise advise that only the person who never lets his guard down, be it with friends or enemies, is never sorry. Worry not and look here, I have cut all the cords but one. As soon as the hunter appears, I will cut this one too, just in time to allow you to escape to save yourself,' responded Palit and continued his slow efforts to cut through the net.

The night passed slowly for the cat. At dawn, both Palit and Lomesh heard the hunter approaching. Soon they could see him walking towards the net.

Lomesh was terrified. He was still not free. But at that precise moment, Palit cut the final cord. Lomesh had no time to waste and he ran as fast as he could to avoid being captured by the hunter. He ran up and took shelter on a branch of the banyan tree. Palit, taking advantage of the situation, escaped into his hole at the foot of the tree.

The hunter saw his net empty and cut to pieces. Disappointed, he picked up the shreds and walked away. But the mouse continued to stay away from the cat. Lomesh tried to assure Palit that he had nothing to fear. 'You have saved my life. You are intelligent. I will not only remain grateful to you but will also devote myself to you now. Please be my friend and guide. Let us continue our friendship. My family and friends will also treat you with respect and cause you no harm,' he promised.

But Palit knew better. 'We became friends only because both of us feared the danger facing us. Friendships forged between the weak and the strong due to mutual but situation-demanded need do not last once the situation changes. Hence, it is important for the weak to remain aware and cautious of the more powerful once the situation reverts to normal. Even if you keep your word, what will stop your family and friends from making me their food, especially if I am easily available to them? You may also harm me any time you are overcome by anger, ego or jealousy. Given how powerful you are compared to me, I will have no way of saving myself. Hence, it is in my interest to maintain distance from you and your family,' he said.

Palit continued, 'He is prudent who knows when to strike an alliance, when to go to war, when to march and when to maintain the status quo. There are no permanent friends, no permanent enemies. We should not trust anyone blindly.'

'About this Shukrāchārya has given two dictums,' Palit added, 'the first is, do not trust one who is not trustworthy and do not trust blindly even those who are trustworthy. Always inspire trust in others but do not put your trust in others. The second dictum is, in all situations, you must strive to protect your own life. Only a person who is alive can even hope for future success. Therefore, it is important for me to protect myself from your species just like you should always protect yourself from the hunter.'

Sharing this astute wisdom, the mouse escaped into his hole.

Be it geopolitics or business or our personal life, this lesson of Bhishma stays relevant to this day.

A king or a leader must always remember that friends and enemies are not permanent, and everyone is looking out for his own interest. A person who is a friend today may go over to the enemy tomorrow and an enemy can become a friend due to aligned interests. A smart leader will use this fact to his advantage. One can find common areas of interest and make an issue-based alliance with one opponent, putting his strengths to full use, thus creating a barrier against another opponent.

A leader must never drop his guard towards both friends and foes and keep a keen watch on all the changes taking place. Playing it smart, the leader can emerge victorious from even the most pressing situations.

Taking the discussion on the topic forward, Bhishma made a very interesting point on Dharma and power. He said:

> When a calamity occurs, the king should not delay his response to it, overthinking the virtue of the necessitated action or lack of it. Because, in such times, it is difficult to clearly differentiate Dharma from Adharma, just like it is not easy to tell footprints of a dog from a wolf. What matters most is the king's ceaseless drive to maintain his power. Only the powerful can attain wealth, army and good ministers. A king without power and wealth is always disregarded. And when his power is strongly rooted in Dharma and truth, the king is protected from all kinds of perils.
>
> I firmly believe attaining power is more important than Dharma. Dharma can be established in the society only by a king who has power. Just like all beings are supported by the earth, Dharma is supported by the power and strength of the king.[134]

Having explained that exceptional measures may be needed to deal with exceptional situations, Bhishma gave one important caveat that drew the line between what is not acceptable even in times of distress.

> Whatever the situation, there should be certain boundaries that must be established which must never be violated. The king should never ally with dacoits even if they are easily available for enlisting in his army for carrying out savage acts.

It is preferable to retire to the forest and live with animals than associate with those who have no moral boundaries.

In fact, even dacoits avoid those people who act mercilessly, without qualms. While dacoits do rob people of their money, they have certain boundaries which they do not transgress in any case, such as raping or violating women, kidnapping young girls, taking away someone else's wife for themselves, killing those who pose no threat, plundering the wealth of Brāhmins, robbing everything from a victim leaving him penniless and hapless, showing ingratitude to those who have helped and continued occupation of villages and towns after having ravaged them.[135]

A point that should be stressed here is that this discourse on Upāya dharma, also called Āpada dharma, is meant for a king or a leader on whose shoulder rests the well-being of a nation-state. It is not applicable to common citizens or even officials and administrators and should not be understood as a free pass to behave as they please for the sake of convenience.

Yuga Dharma

Yudhishthira asked another poignant question about the policy to be adopted by a king as yugas changed from Sat to Tretā to Dwāpar to Kali, righteousness began to deteriorate and criminals abounded.[136]

'In such times, the king should follow the policy of Āpada dharma without being carried away with idealism, keeping aversion at bay and acting according to the demands of the situation,' said Bhishma and narrated a conversation between King Shatrunjaya of Sauvirdesha and Rishi Bhāradvāja.[137]

Bhishma said that one day Shatrunjaya approached Rishi Bhāradvāja and sought his guidance on obtaining a position of power and retaining it in hostile situations wherein crooks and the unrighteous have become strong and prominent. Rishi Bhāradvāja shared a few tips on governance, diplomacy and polity in response:

> A king who wishes to establish and uphold his power should always be ready to give danda without hesitation—punish the offenders, establish the rule of law and display his authority, as the situation demands. It is through punishment that the subjects can be disciplined and made to follow the law of the land.
>
> The king must be extremely cautious and not let his opponents find any chinks in his armour. But he must proactively look out for the flaws and weaknesses of his opponents and exploit them to his advantage.

When dealing with a troublesome enemy (internal and external), the king should ensure the enemy's rout is total, from their very root—मूलच्छेद (moolaccheda). Once the root is destroyed, all dependent on it and supported by it will also be destroyed. If the enemy's allies don't fall in line by themselves, they should be destroyed too. A person who does not destroy the enemy even after overpowering him, calls upon his own death.

The shloka quoted by Bhishma is very well known and is given below:

ऋणशेषाग्निशेषं च शत्रुशेषं तथैव च ।
पुनः पुनः प्रवर्धन्ते तस्माच्छेषं न कारयेत् ।।

Three things, if not completely eradicated in time, will keep growing and causing trouble—debt, fire and an enemy. Hence, even a very small amount of these should not be allowed to fester.

When faced with a war, strategise smartly, fight with valour on the battlefield and if need be, find an escape route to run away smartly.

Always be sweet in speech and polite in behaviour, giving up anger, but only overtly. In actions, be ruthless. Agree to compromise and settlement if the situation demands, but do not trust the opponent fully. Use the opportunity to protect your interest and escape, but don't let your guard down. The person who rests reassured after reaching a settlement with the opponent is as foolish as one who falls into a deep sleep on a branch of the tree. Falling off is imminent in both situations.

A smart person bows to the enemy, reassures and even comforts him and earns his trust when the odds are stacked against him, but remains alert and destroys the enemy when the opportunity presents itself.

A person should have the ability to act blind or deaf and pretend to see or hear nothing if that is the need of the hour. Heroism should be shown only when the time and place are appropriate and in your favour, considering your own strengths and weaknesses and those of the opponent. A task, however noble, if undertaken when the time is not right, rarely gets the desired results.

Being cautious and circumspect, the king should attempt to avoid a calamity which hasn't yet occurred but is likely. However, if it does occur, then it is obligatory for the king to courageously deal with it and if required, face the enemy with grit and courage.

Using spies effectively in his own territory as well as in enemy territory, the king should proactively identify and weed out spies of the enemy operating against his interests.

A king should trust not those who are untrustworthy and be circumspect of even those who are otherwise trustworthy. This is because when trusted ones turn rogue, they have the potential to completely destroy the king as they have access to confidential information about the king as well as acquaintance with people close to the king.

The king should kill even a father or a son or a brother if they create obstacles for him and the kingdom. Nor should he hesitate to punish a teacher who has gone astray and tried to rebel against the State. And he should never show compassion to a person who has caused him or the kingdom harm in the past.

While subjugating the enemy, a king must also seek to shower favours on people who support him and expand his sphere of influence by getting other allies.

It is never wise to give up on tasks that are going to result in gains in the present in the hope of something that will yield results in the unknown future.

A king should have an eagle-like vision to see far enough, a heron-like focus on the target, the caution of a dog, the valour of a lion, the suspicion of a crow and the approach of a snake. Like a snake that enters the hole when his prey is hidden inside and destroys it, the king should also exploit the flaws of his opponent and subjugate him. He should do all this with an unagitated mind.

A rule of thumb to remember—bow to the more courageous and powerful, threaten and subjugate the timid, buy out the greedy and fight with the one who is equivalent in strength.

Do not enter a river you can't cross, do not seize the wealth that can be taken back by the enemy forcefully, do not dig at the base of the tree (or enemy) that you cannot fully uproot, do not try to kill him whom you do not have the power to behead.

Having said all this, please bear in mind that such measures are to be implemented when faced with existential crises or opponents who are cruel. These measures are not to be resorted to when you are capable enough of dealing with challenges righteously and the times are not desperate.

Bhishma too, like Rishi Bharadvāja, recognised that actions resorted to for gaining power in dire conditions may, strictly speaking, fall in the unrighteous category. That is not the precedent that the king must aspire to set for the society, even if that was the best course of action in the specific circumstances. Bhishma did not want Āpada dharma to become a norm that could be used for the sake of convenience for the king to have his way. Hence, Bhishma very clearly adds a caveat that even if done in desperate times, the king should be aware of his unrighteous action and do prāyaschitta—seek atonement—when the situation stabilises, by performing the requisite rituals and imbibing virtues in mind, speech and action.[138]

A Tryst with Hunger

'How far can a king go in terms of comprising with what is impermissible in calamitous times?' asked Yudhishthira. He then made his question more specific, 'If the going gets tough and the situation is desperate, especially for a Brāhmin, how should he deal with it?'

The reference specifically to a Brāhmin is also because the restrictions on lifestyle prescribed by the scriptures for Brāhmins are a lot more stringent in terms of what to eat and not to eat, what is the permissible mode of earning and what is not and so on. Yudhishthira wanted to know if such concessions were available to Brāhmins too in difficult times.

'In such times, Brāhmins must be guided by their wisdom. Let me tell you what Rishi Vishvāmitra did when he faced misfortune,' said Bhishma and narrated the story he had heard from his elders and gurus.[139]

Once upon a time, rains failed the earth for twelve years in succession. The drought was so severe that people started dying of hunger and thirst. There was destruction all around. Rishi Vishvāmitra was also a victim of this wrath of nature. For days together, he went without food and water. But how many days can a person survive like that? Vishvāmitra's health began to deteriorate, and he felt so weak that he thought he would die if he did not have food for a few days more. He went from place to place in search of food but in vain. His search then took him to a place where the chāndālas lived. In one of the huts of the chāndālas, Vishvāmitra saw a discarded piece of meat from a dog's thigh. He made up his mind to steal and eat it after ensuring the chāndāla in the house was asleep.

When Vishvāmitra went to fetch the piece of meat, the movement outside the door woke up the chāndāla. He opened the door and enquired about the reason for the rishi's presence and was shocked to hear that the rishi wanted the dog meat. 'Dog meat is forbidden for Brāhmins. And even in dog meat, the thigh is considered the most unsuitable. Why do you wish to destroy the punya you have accumulated by tapasyā of so many years? It doesn't befit someone like you to crave such food,' the chāndāla told Vishvāmitra.

Vishvāmitra was unmoved. His mind was made up. 'At this point, I must eat whatever is available.

I can gain back the punya by undertaking stringent tapasyā only if I live to see another day. I don't crave the meat for what it is but only as something that will keep me alive. I see nothing wrong with that. When survival is at risk, arguing about what is edible and what is not is not the wisest thing to do. Scriptures allow for exceptions when a life is in danger,' asserted Vishvāmitra.

The chāndāla continued his protestations for a while, hoping to discourage the rishi from committing such an abominable sin, but to no avail. Finally, he gave in and handed the piece of dog meat to Vishvāmitra.

Rishi Vishvāmitra went back to his hut and cooked the meat himself. And like he always did before each meal, he made offerings of the food to the gods and the forefathers.

It is said Vishvāmitra didn't have to eat the dog meat as Indra deva was so pleased with his understanding of Dharma that even before the rishi picked up the meat to eat it, Indra deva ended the drought and rains nourished the earth once again.

'Even when the situation is as bad as it was for Rishi Vishvāmitra, a wise person should not lose hope. He should do whatever he can to emerge out of the adversity, relying on his intelligence and discernment to determine what is doable and what is not in that situation,' concluded Bhishma.

Morality of Āpada Dharma

The story of Vishvāmitra disheartened Yudhishthira. 'If such transgressions, which are akin to falsehood, are being advised as permissible, what actions should

I really shun? Even dacoits have some boundaries drawn, as you mentioned. Where does a king draw a line? I feel distraught and deluded. My enthusiasm to live by the tenets of Dharma has reduced. I can't get myself to act in accordance with what you have said,' said Yudhishthira sadly.

Bhishma looked at Yudhishthira lovingly. He understood the struggle going on inside his heart and mind. Balancing morality and pragmatism is a very thin and tight rope to walk on. He spoke comfortingly:

> All that I have shared with you is not just based on the scriptures, it also contains the wisdom gathered by wise persons through their experience, just like honey collected by honeybees from different flowers. Kings cannot traverse this world with only a singular morality. They need to employ different tactics to effectively navigate different situations based on wisdom imbibed from various sources of knowledge.
>
> Dharma springs from wisdom and manifests itself in the conduct of a wise person. A king endowed with superior intelligence and desirous of victory establishes Dharma in the society, aided by the wisdom gained from the scriptures as well as the experiences of the wise. He cannot govern a kingdom without understanding the subtleties and nuances of Dharma.
>
> Dharma sometimes appears as Adharma and Adharma seems to take the form of Dharma. A person who doesn't understand this, never having encountered such a complex and confounding situation earlier, is left perplexed and confused when faced with one. Hence, you must gain an understanding of such situations beforehand and

implement the lessons as appropriate when the occasion arises.

You must seek to gain this wisdom from those who possess true knowledge. There are many who sound smart but are devoid of wisdom. You will have to learn to distinguish between the genuinely wise and the impostors. People who preach the futility of scriptures or find only faults in them must most definitely be shunned, as well as those who seek knowledge only for the sake of making a living, along with those who are wicked and immature.

Guru Brihaspati is of the view that Dharma cannot be understood only by intelligence or only by words contained in the scriptures. It is through the congruence of both scriptural wisdom and intelligence that Dharma has to be understood.

You should not forget that you are a Kshatriya and a king. You will have to undertake violent actions to ensure order and justice. Not killing a person who deserves to be killed is as sinful as killing the underserving. It is only through severe actions can a king maintain order and discipline in the society, otherwise anarchy is unavoidable. A king in whose kingdom criminals abound causing harm to innocent public is a blot on Kshatriyas.

In times of distress, it is necessary for a king to do all he can to protect the innocent and punish the wicked. The Dharma ordained for kings is no doubt arduous. Hence, remaining steadfast in Rāja dharma, govern your kingdom as you must. While doing so, ensure persons of wisdom and learning are by your side and well respected by you.[140]

Yudhishthira listened to Bhishma's advice intently. The cobwebs of confusion that had formed in his mind due to the grief of war gradually started getting cleared.

Where Should We Draw the Line?

Yudhishthira's question to Bhishma is very pertinent. Exceptional situations call for exceptional approaches, but where should we draw the line? What are the non-negotiables that we determine for ourselves, those that are sacrosanct, come what may?

Bhishma seems to imply that there is no one answer to that question. We have to weigh the scope of our influence, that is, fully understand the potential consequences of both our action and our inaction in that particular situation on ourselves and on those affected by our actions and then take a decision. Vidura suggests 'आत्मार्थे पृथ्वीं त्यजेत—For the sake of your ātmā, sacrifice even this earth'. He seems to say, do that which you do not feel guilty about, that which you will not eventually regret.

But how do we know if that is indeed the right mode of action at that point in time. This is what 'Dharma sankata' is all about. Krishna expounded the Srimad Bhagavad Geetā to help Arjuna navigate such an ethical dilemma. His advice is to develop 'yogastha buddhi', that intellect not tainted by biases, and you will know what you should do.

How does one develop yogastha buddhi? Study the Srimad Bhagavad Geetā!

ॐ

Thirteen Powerful Foes

Yudhishthira's and Bhishma's discussions now veered towards individual vices and virtues. They had already spoken about the need for self-restraint and how all virtues practically emerge from that.[141]

Yudhishthira then asked about human frailties. 'What gives rise to anger (क्रोध), lust (काम), sorrow (शोक), delusion (मोह), desire to do what is proscribed (विधित्सा), unkindness (परासुता), pride (मद), greed (लोभ), malice (मात्सर्य), ill will (असूया), contempt (कुत्सा), jealousy (ईर्ष्या) and miserliness (कृपण). Please tell me about these in detail.'

'Yudhishthira, these thirteen frailties that you mentioned are very powerful foes of all creatures. They besiege and entice people in every way. They afflict an ignorant person and goad him into submission. And then they seize him thoroughly like wolves ravish their prey. They push a person into committing sinful actions and bring immense grief to him and those near him. Everyone must necessarily know about these stubborn thirteen foes,' said Bhishma and explained in detail their origin and their antidotes.[142]

His answer is summed up in the table below.

Vice	Originates from	Can be destroyed by
Anger (क्रोध)	Covetousness increases due to the tendency to find fault in others	Cultivating a sense of forgiveness
Lust (काम)	Conception of a desire that is further strengthened by indulgence	Resolutely turning away from it

Vice	Originates from	Can be destroyed by
Delusion (मोह)	Ignorance, which is further exacerbated by incessant engagement in that activity	Counsel and company of wise persons
Sorrow (शोक)	Loss of someone or something that is loved	Understanding that no one and nothing stays forever, therefore grieving over loss is to no avail
Desire to do what is proscribed (विधित्सा)	Reading scriptures antagonistic to Dharma	Acquiring the right knowledge
Unkindness (परासुता)	Anger, greed and finding faults in others	Developing compassion and detachment towards all and gaining the right knowledge
Pride (मद)	Attachment for one's stature, learning or prosperity	Understanding of the true nature—the impermanence of this body and ever-changing time
Greed (लोभ)	Ignorance	Understanding the ephemerality of material things
Malice (मात्सर्य)	Company of wicked people and ignorance	Service of the wise and virtuous
Ill will (असूया)	Inability to avenge the wrong done to self by someone more powerful	Cultivating kindness
Abusiveness (कुत्सा)	Influence of the words of the uncivil	Keeping company of the virtuous
Jealousy (ईर्ष्या)	Seeing joy of others and desiring the same	Developing wisdom and discernment

Vice	Originates from	Can be destroyed by
Meanness (कृपण)	Influence/company of mean and wretched people	Understanding of the strength of virtue

'All these foes can be subdued by quietening one's mind. The Kauravas were afflicted with all thirteen. You, on the other hand, were always rooted in truth. You achieved this focus by serving the wise and the noble. Therefore, you managed to conquer these foes,' Bhishma told Yudhishthira appreciatingly.

Raibhya and Yavakreeta: A Tale of Jealousy, Lust, Anger and Ruin

The interplay of the thirteen foes which predominantly arise out of kāma and krodha can lead to destructive consequences even for wise persons if they don't remain aware of them. Even a momentary loss of awareness can lead to these foes taking possession of the person and making him or her act in ways they would regret later.

This destructive interplay is illustrated in the story of Raibhya muni and Yavakreeta. Although this story is not from Shānti Parva and not narrated by Bhishma, mentioning it here is apt as it clearly brings out why these thirteen traits are foes. The story given here was narrated by Rishi Lomasha to the Pāndavas when they were still in vanvās.[143]

Once there lived two friends, Raibhya muni and Rishi Bharadvāja, in a place called Kardamila. Raibhya had two sons, Arvāvasu and Parāvasu. Bharadvāja had one son by the name of Yavakreeta.

Raibhya was a very learned man, so were his sons. Their fame was spread wide. Bharadvāja, on the other hand, was always more involved in his tapasyā. As fewer people knew him, he would not get the kind of reception and respect that Raibhya would due to the latter's deep knowledge of scriptures. This disparity did not trouble Bharadvāja as he was happy with the path of austerity which he himself had chosen.

But that was not so for Yavakreeta. Raibhya's popularity and its lack for his father would agitate him. One day, in a fit of jealousy, he decided to acquire knowledge of the Vedas like Raibhya's sons. But he did not have the patience to follow the process of learning, as students must, from a guru. Yavakreeta wanted to gain all the knowledge as quickly as he could. He decided to undertake intense tapasyā to appease Indra deva and acquire the knowledge.

Stirred by Yavakreeta's severe austerity, Indra appeared to him and asked the reason for performing such intense tapasyā.

'Indra deva, I wish to obtain the knowledge of the Vedas without having to study them. It will take me a long time to learn them if I have to sit at a guru's feet. I wish to gain the wisdom quickly and I want this tapasyā to help me achieve that,' said Yavakreeta.

Indra was not convinced. 'This is not the right approach to study the Vedas. Why do you wish to circumvent the path of learning? Go and seek the wisdom of the Vedas at the feet of some suitable teacher,' said Indra and left.

Yavakreeta was not discouraged by Indra's response. He doubled down on his tapasyā. When his tapasyā reached a peak, Indra came again and tried to instil sense in Yavakreeta. 'This desire of yours is unreasonable and unwise. You will not achieve your goal with this approach.'

Yavakreeta was adamant. 'If you do not fulfil my desire, I will intensify my tapasyā even more. I will offer parts of my body one by one to the fire,' he said.

To discourage Yavakreeta, Indra thought of an idea. He took the form of a very old rishi, afflicted by tuberculosis. One morning when Yavakreeta went for his ablutions by the bank of the Gangā, he saw an old rishi throwing fistful of sand in the river. Amused, he enquired the reason for the rishi's actions.

'I wish to build a bridge across the river,' replied the rishi coolly. Yavakreeta couldn't control his laughter. 'This is a huge river with a strong flow of water. You will never accomplish what you've set out to. It is a futile attempt. Please don't waste your time—take up something that you can actually accomplish,' he said.

Now it was the rishi's turn to smile. 'Is my action as futile as your attempt to obtain the wisdom of the Vedas without making the effort to study them thoroughly?' he asked.

Yavakreeta immediately realised that the rishi was actually Indra. 'If you think my tapasyā is as futile as your efforts to build a bridge, I'll request you to grant me what is possible. Please grant me that by which I become respected and well-known more than others in this world,' he said.

Indra then relented. 'So be it. May you and your father gain the knowledge of the Vedas and may other desires of yours be fulfilled,' pronounced the wise Indra. Yavakreeta couldn't believe his good fortune. Excited, he went looking for his father and broke the news of Indra's boon to him.

Bharadvāja, his father, however, wasn't too pleased. He was a man of wisdom and experience. He sounded a word of caution, 'Gaining knowledge in this manner without proper effort and approach will only make you arrogant. Do remember, arrogance destroys the person and everything he has.' He narrated a story to his son to drill into him the need to be watchful of his attitude lest the boon becomes a bane.

Once upon a time a rishi named Balādhi, reeling under the grief of the death of his young son, undertook a severe penance to obtain another son who was immortal like the gods. The gods did bless him with a son but said, 'Anyone who is born must die, a human being cannot have the longevity of the gods.'

'All right, then bless my son with a long life. Let him live as long as these mountains stand,' requested Balādhi. The Devatās obliged.

Balādhi's son was very intelligent and hence was named Medhāvi, the intelligent one. Due to the boon given to him, Medhāvi became fearless. He would use his intelligence to trouble the rishis and the people around him. He did not fear death or adverse repercussions that could destroy him because he knew he would live as long as the mountains stood. Day by day, he became more and more arrogant and rash.

One day, intoxicated with arrogance, he confronted and insulted a very accomplished rishi called Dhanushāksha. Furious at the unwarranted aggression and humiliation, Dhanushāksha cursed him that he would turn into ashes. But nothing happened. Medhāvi laughed disparagingly. Dhanushāksha looked at him closely and observed that there was no indication on him of weathering that came with age. Through the strength of his tapasyā, he realised the source of Medhāvi's longevity and arrogance and decided to teach him a lesson. He engaged many extremely well-nourished and powerful buffaloes to start breaking up the mountains standing there. As the mountains began to reduce in size, Medhāvi's health began to deteriorate and eventually he collapsed, dead.

Balādhi's father was inconsolable. The rishis gathered there consoled him. 'No one can defy the laws of nature. Humans are meant to die and that will come true anyhow, just like Dhanushāksha found a way to crush the mountains with buffaloes,' they said, wisely.

'This is how young ones fall prey to destruction due to their arrogance, fuelled by such unwise boons. Therefore, you should now be very careful. Most importantly, keep away from Raibhya. He has a bad temper and can cause harm to you if provoked,' instructed Bharadvāja.

'Don't worry, Father. I will do as you say. Raibhya muni is also like a father to me,' assured Yavakreeta. But it was just a matter of time before pride started engulfing him. He began to derive pleasure from challenging and troubling other rishis in the forest due to the knowledge that had just come to him without putting in the necessary time and effort.

Acquiring knowledge is just one end goal of learning, the other and the more important one is developing character and perspective. Yavakreeta had gained one but was thoroughly lacking in the other.

With each passing day, as the other rishis avoided confronting him, Yavakreeta became more and more fearless and brash. One day, while passing by the āshrama of Raibhya, he saw Raibhya's beautiful daughter-in-law, who was Parāvasu's wife. Overcome with lust, he lost all sense of propriety. He shamelessly accosted her and spoke in a tone of entitlement, 'Hey beautiful, come and serve me.'

The lady was shocked and embarrassed. She feared openly disobeying Yavakreeta, afraid of his curse. She was also aware of Raibhya's powers. Unwillingly and in tears, she agreed. Yavakreeta led her to an isolated place in the āshrama. Raibhya returned just then and was shocked to see his daughter-in-law sobbing helplessly. He was even more shocked to find Yavakreeta there. The daughter-in-law told Raibhya about Yavakreeta's indecent proposal. Raibhya's anger seemed to have no bounds, as if the fire of anger was burning him from the inside. He cursed Yavakreeta to death. As Raibhya was a very accomplished rishi, his curse came into effect shortly afterwards and Yavakreeta met his death.

When Bharadvāja heard of his son's death, he was beyond himself. Wise and mature that he otherwise was, the grief of the death of his only son, who meant everything to him, was overpowering. In that moment of intense grief, he cursed Raibhya to death at the hands of his own son.

But having pronounced the curse, Bharadvāja, who was already engulfed by sorrow, was now overcome with an intense bout of guilt. He realised he had thoughtlessly cursed his friend. Unable to handle so much sorrow and guilt, he entered the burning pyre of his son and gave up his life.

Of the impact of his curse, Raibhya's son Parāvasu accidentally killed his father, mistaking him for a wild animal.

This is how the interplay of jealousy, greed, arrogance, lust, anger and attachment destroyed two families of learned rishis.

It is said that Arvāvasu, Raibhya's other son, was an epitome of truth and kindness and one who had achieved control over his senses. He successfully undertook severe penance and brought back to life his father as well as Bharadvāja and Yavakreeta.

ॐ

Wisdom, the Ultimate Refuge

'Pitāmaha, what would you say is the ultimate refuge of human beings—relatives, rituals, wealth or wisdom?' asked Yudhishthira.

'Wisdom is the ultimate refuge of all human beings. Wisdom is the greatest acquisition a person can have. Through wisdom, a person can achieve lasting happiness. Through wisdom, a person can attain heaven. Great people have achieved success and prosperity through wisdom. It is through wisdom that fortunes can be turned around,' said Bhishma and narrated an interesting conversation between Indra deva and Kāshyapa to support his answer.[144]

> Once upon a time, Kāshyapa, who was the son of a humble rishi, was insulted and pushed out of a chariot by a wealthy trader over some argument. Kāshyapa felt humiliated and was extremely upset and angry. Unable to bear the dishonour, he decided to give up his life. 'I see no purpose in the life of a destitute. It is better for me to die than live in such poverty and face humiliation,' he thought to himself as he sat still in the same spot where he had fallen off the chariot.
>
> After some time, a fox came his way and initiated a conversation. 'There are so many species of living creatures in this world. They all aspire to be born as human beings. It is only through good karma that this human birth is possible. You have been born as a human and have been endowed with intelligence. Why do you then dislike yourself so much that you wish to give up your life? Isn't it ego that is making you act this way?' asked the fox from him.

Kāshyapa was taken aback on seeing a fox who spoke like a human being. But he didn't react. The fox continued his monologue. 'I consider even those with hands extremely fortunate. I envy their luck. Like you crave for wealth, I crave for a pair of hands. There is no greater wealth I can think of than that. Because I have no hands, I am unable to pull out thorns from my body, nor am I able to turn away the small insects biting me. Look at you humans! With hands, you are capable of yoking mighty bulls to a cart and ride it.'

The fox continued, 'You can't even begin to imagine the pain which animals go through because they do not have hands or the ability to communicate like humans. You must consider yourself privileged that you are not a fox like me, or a mouse, snake, bug, frog—or any such animal. You should be happy and content being a human. Look how helpless I am before this tiny bug. It is sucking my blood but I can't do anything to stop it. The only reason I do not commit suicide is because killing oneself incurs great sin. And when I look around, I don't see anyone who is the epitome of perfect happiness and has no reason to complain. No one is fully satisfied with what they have—there is always something one wants. Desire is like the fire that blazes when more fuel is added to it. Fulfilment of one desire only leads to more desires.'

'Even in humans, I see many who go through hard times in life and end up committing forbidden acts. There are some who are relegated as outcastes, some who have disabilities and some are prone to diseases. Yet, they continue to face life and do not consider suicide as an escape route. You have a healthy body and are free of disease; your limbs are perfectly strong.

Give up this sinful thought and engage yourself in activities befitting you,' advised the fox.

The fox added, 'Although I am a fox, I attempt to live my life in a way that I can be born as a human in the next birth. As a human, I wish to engage myself in study and tapasyā to gain knowledge and wisdom of what is worth having and what should be given away.'

Kāshyapa was astonished at these wise words of the fox. 'But how can a fox have such wisdom and speak like this?' he wondered, going into deep meditation. It was then that he realised that the fox was Indra deva himself. A strong message had been conveyed and received. Giving up his plan to die, Kāshyapa got up and headed back to his āshrama.

Wealth will come and go, relatives might turn their backs on us, the results of our actions are not completely in our control. Nonetheless, however dire the situation, with the help of wisdom, we will find a way to cope with it.

With wisdom, we can gain wealth, manage relations, perform the right actions and, most importantly, develop the right perspective to accept life with all its ups and downs. For the wise know एतदपि गमिष्यति—this too shall pass.[145] It is wisdom that helps a person differentiate between a worthwhile pursuit and a vain effort.

This is the purport of Indra's message to Kāshyapa and of Bhishma's to Yudhishthira.

ॐ

The Karma Principle

The conversation between Yudhishthira and Bhishma veered to topics beyond Rāja dharma. Yudhishthira asked all sorts of questions and Bhishma provided him the answers. All this time, Yudhishthira's mind wasn't completely at peace. The sight of his Pitāmaha lying before him on a bed of arrows kept his grief and guilt simmering.

He expressed his sorrow to his grandfather. 'Your discourse has been enlightening but my heart finds no peace. When I see you fallen like this, covered in blood, your body thoroughly ripped apart by these arrows, I become acutely aware of the sin that I have committed. So many mighty warriors, kings and princes have been killed in this war. All the sons of Dhritarāshtra have been annihilated. I hold myself guilty for this destruction. I consider Duryodhana to be luckier than me. He died fighting in the war, a death befitting of a warrior. And I am left here, looking at all this carnage brought about by no one but me. Please instruct me on how I can atone for my sins and find peace in this world and beyond.'

'Why do you hold yourself responsible for actions over which you had little control?' asked Bhishma. He spoke with a lot of empathy and narrated another story to Yudhishthira.[146]

There was once an old woman named Gautami. Her only support in life was her son. One day she found her son dead. A snake had bitten him. As she grieved sitting beside her son's body, her neighbour came by. This neighbour was a hunter by profession. His name was Arjunaka. He had come to meet Gautami and was shocked to see her son's dead body, bitten by a snake. He looked around and found that the snake that had bitten the boy was still in the vicinity. Immediately, he ran after the snake and caught it. To cheer up Gautami, he showed her the captured snake and said, 'This snake is your culprit. He is the killer of your son. Tell me how do you wish to see it die? Should I roast it on fire or cut it into tiny pieces?'

'Arjunaka, please set this snake free,' replied Gautami. 'No one can avert what is destined. My son will not come back to life if you kill the snake. Then why do you wish to commit the sin of killing a living creature?' she asked calmly. Arjunaka was surprised. He tried to convince Gautami to let him kill the snake, but the old woman did not budge.

The snake that had been caught was getting restless. Its body was in pain. It spoke slowly, addressing Arjunaka, 'Why do you hold me responsible for the boy's death? I did not bite him of my own volition. My action was under the influence of Mrityu—death. I have no power to resist death's will. I bit the boy under Mrityu's instruction, not out of any personal anger, greed or grudge. I am nothing more than an instrument in this outcome. I am like a potter's wheel. A potter's wheel has no free will. It is subservient to the potter's wishes. It cannot be considered a doer. So, if you must hold anyone responsible for the boy's death, it must be Mrityu.'

The hunter dismissed the snake's pleadings. 'Even if you consider yourself only as an instrument, you are still the offender. By your argument, every criminal will rationalise his crime and attempt to absolve himself,' he said. But the snake insisted it was not to be blamed as it was only an agent working without any personal motivation.

When they were arguing, Mrityu himself appeared and pleaded not guilty. He presented the same logic as that of the snake to prove his innocence. 'I didn't ask the snake to bite the boy of my own will. I was only following the instructions of the powerful Kāla.[147] The way the clouds get dispersed here and there by the force of the wind, not by their own accord, my actions are subject to the commands of Kāla. Every being and everything in this universe is under Kāla's influence,' he said.

Hearing his name, Kāla came to the spot. He too pleaded his innocence in the matter of the boy's death. 'Neither I, nor Mrityu, nor the snake are responsible for the boy's death. The cause of the boy's death is his own karma. His own karma has led to his destruction. We have just been instruments of the same. Just like a potter shapes the mound of clay in whatever form he wishes, a person shapes his life with his own karma. A person's karma follows him everywhere, even in death,' said Kāla.

Gautami agreed completely with Kāla. She repeated his words that the cause of her son's death was his own karma. She requested Arjunaka to set the snake free. The hunter was left with no arguments. He let the snake go.

'Yudhishthira, understand this story and do not grieve. Let go of your sorrow as Gautami did after the death of her son. Duryodhana has met the end he deserved,' Bhishma concluded.

Karma and Kartā Bhāva

When Arjuna was under a delusion just before the Kurukshetra war, Krishna expounded the Geetā to him. In that, Krishna, in his Vishwarupa avatāra, told him:

मयैवैते निहता: पूर्वमेव
निमित्तमात्रं भव सव्यसाचिन् ।।

(Your cousins) have already been killed by me, you become just an instrument of (my will).

The verse says that the end of Kauravas and their allies was predestined due to their karmas. The Pāndavas were only the instruments that produced the outcome.

While this line of thought is very potent to discourage people from indulging in actions that lead to negative karma, it could also be used to rationalise any action by those not given to using discerning buddhi. The hunter does have a point when he tells the snake that the instrumentality argument can be used by any criminal to escape punishment.

How can we make sense of this profound lesson without falling back on convenient but incorrect conclusions?

The answer lies in the comment of the snake where it says that its action was not motivated by any of its emotions—neither anger, nor grudge nor greed, but just driven by what the situation demanded at that moment. In that sense, the snake's, Mrityu's and Kāla's role must be seen as that of the executioner in the gallows. The executioner implements the death sentence pronounced on the criminal as a matter of duty, not out of any personal grudge or enmity.

This is what Krishna means when, in Srimad Bhagavad Geetā, he tells Arjuna to give up the kartā bhāva—to give up ownership of action. Krishna says that we must act because swadharma requires us to do so as a call of duty, and not because we are driven by impulses of desire, lust, anger, greed, ego or hatred. Rather, we must be guided by objectivity and wisdom.

ॐ

Purushārtha versus Fortune

'Pitāmaha, which of the two—purushārtha (enterprise/industriousness) or fortune—is greater according to you?' asked Yudhishthira.

'Once upon a time, Rishi Vashishtha asked exactly this question to Brahma deva. Let me narrate to you the answer which Brahma deva gave,' said Bhishma, reminiscing.[148]

> There is nothing born without a seed. Without the seed, there is no fruit. From the seed itself a seed is obtained and so is obtained a fruit. The quality of the crop that a farmer reaps from his farm is a result of the quality of the seed he sows. However, there is no crop unless a seed is sown in a tilled and fertile soil that facilitates the sprouting of the seed. Likewise, without enterprise and effort, fortune alone cannot produce any result. Our actions are like the tilled soil and fortune is like the seed. The outcome is the result of the union of the seed and the soil.
>
> The doer experiences the fruit of his actions—in material form and in spirit, both good and bad. Only when a person acts does fortune come into play and the result is achieved. Without action, no result is ever produced. It is only through appropriate enterprise that a person attains prosperity and heaven.
>
> The purushārtha of a person does fructify according to his fortune but without effort, fortune by itself has nothing to offer. Fortune has roots in our actions. Sometimes we see that a wicked person gets to enjoy many pleasures in life and we wonder why. That person is probably reaping the fruits of his

past actions. Rest assured, such pleasures never last for long.

We must always remember that a person's ātmā itself is his best friend and, at the same time, his worst enemy. The ātmā is a witness to all the actions and inactions of the person.

Fortune is like the fire which, when fanned by human effort, becomes even more powerful and diminishes when the fuel depletes. Fortune by itself isn't sufficiently potent to produce results for a person who is averse to enterprise. Like a student follows his guru, fortune too follows purushārtha.

Thus, I have shared with you my insights on the fruits of purushārtha. It is through the influence of fortune and diligent enterprise as ordained by scriptures that a person eventually attains heaven.

'However, even fortune cannot save a person who is completely deluded and enslaved by his senses,' said Bhishma.

Factors of Success

In Adhyaya 18 of Srimad Bhagavad Geetā, Krishna explains five factors for success. He says:

अधिष्ठानं तथा कर्ता करणं च पृथग्विधम्।
विविधाश्च पृथक्चेष्टा दैवं चैवात्र पञ्चमम्।।18.14।।

The five factors are अधिष्ठानं (adhishthanam)—the locus of action, कर्ता (kartā)—the doer, करणं (karanam)—various resources and instruments used, पृथक्चेष्टा (prithakcheshtā)—different actions and processes and दैवं (daivam)—fortune.

The first four factors that Krishna mentions are in control of the doer and hence form the purushārtha. Fortune matters, but it is not the only factor. Thus, Krishna too agrees that fortune cannot function in isolation. It comes into play only when purushārtha is performed by the individual.

ॐ

A Thousand Names for Moksha

Yudhishthira's and Bhishma's discussion covered every aspect of practical and personal Dharma. Yudhishthira's questions swerved to theology, metaphysics and spirituality. He enquired about philosophies such as Sānkhya and Yoga and had questions on topics such as the creation of the universe, the nature of truth and reality, pāpa–punya and their consequences, rebirth, the importance of giving and so on.

Bhishma answered all the questions with patience, narrating anecdotes and stories from the ancient past to explain his position and views.

Yudhishthira listened very attentively to all that Bhishma said. Then, he had one more question. He wished to know if there was any one particular thing that could release people from the cycle of birth-and-death, something that would be accessible to everyone.

He asked, 'Who is the ultimate refuge? Which is the foremost Dharma? How can a person break free of this cycle of birth and death?'

Bhishma closed his eyes as if in contemplation and then spoke as if he was in a trance:

> By chanting the thousand names of him who is the master of the universe, the lord of the gods, the eternal one, we can achieve prosperity and happiness. Worship that unchanging one. Sing his praise, meditate on him and bow down to him. All sorrows melt away of the person who sings the praise of the

Lord, with the mind fixed intently on him. He is omnipresent, without a beginning or an end. He is the cause of the origin of all beings.

To sing his name and worship him is the foremost Dharma.

He is Vishnu. He is Pundarikāsha—the lotus-eyed one. That Vishnu is the ultimate refuge of all, the purest amongst the pure, the most auspicious amongst the auspicious, the lord of the gods and the father of all beings. From him, all emerged at the beginning of time and in him, the world dissolves in the end.

Listen carefully as I tell you his thousand names. Chanting these names removes all fear. These names describe his gunas[149] that have been sung by the rishis.

Bhishma then recited one of the most powerful and sacred stotras[150] of Vishnu, the *Vishnu Sahasranāma*—the thousand names of Vishnu. Yudhishthira and everyone present there heard Bhishma chant *Vishnu Sahasranāma*, enraptured.[151]

Earlier in the conversation, Yudhishthira had requested Bhishma to tell him more about Shiva.

'I am not capable of talking about the glory of Shiva. He is omnipresent and the creator of all gods. He is beyond both prakriti (matter) and purusha (consciousness). Only Krishna, due to his eternal Shiva-bhakti spanning over lifetimes can speak of the

Mahādeva,' replied Bhishma and requested Krishna to respond to Yudhishthira's question.

Krishna recounted the boon-giving and desire-fulfilling thousand names of Shiva, the *Shiva Sahasranāma*.[152] This strotra was revealed to Maharshi Tandi by Brahma deva himself. Maharshi Tandi brought this hymn to the people of the world. And it was told to Krishna by Rishi Upamanyu, an ardent devotee of Bhagavāna Shiva.

Shiva and Vishnu Are One

There is a tendency amongst some modern-day historians to present Shaivism and Vaishnavism as being antagonistic to each other. There are, however, innumerable examples in history to debunk such narratives. Several Shaiva kings have patronised Vishnu temples and vice versa. The simultaneous and symbiotic existence of Vaishnava and Shaiva schools of philosophy is quite prominent in our itihāsa too, as can be seen in the Mahābhārata itself where Shiva and Vishnu are given equal prominence.

There are verses in Harivamsha Parva (2.125.29, 2.125.41) as well as in other texts like Padma Purāna (2.71.20) that deserve a mention here. These verses posit the one-ness of Shiva and Vishnu.

शिवाय विष्णुरूपाय विष्णवे शिवरूपिणे ।
यथान्तरं न पश्यामि तेन तौ दिशतः शिवम् ।।

Shiva in the form of Vishnu and Vishnu in the form of Shiva. I see no difference between them, they both bestow auspiciousness.

रुद्रस्य परमो विष्णुर्विष्णोश्च परमः शिवः ।
एक एव द्विधा भूतो लोके चरति नित्यशः ।।

Vishnu is the supreme lord of Rudra (Shiva) and Rudra is the supreme lord of Vishnu. These are but one traversing the world in two forms.

शिवाय विष्णुरूपाय शिवरूपाय विष्णवे ।
शिवस्य हृदयं विष्णुः विष्णोश्च हृदयं शिवः ।।

Shiva in the form of Vishnu and Vishnu in the form of Shiva. Vishnu resides in the heart of Shiva and Shiva resides in the heart of Vishnu.

ॐ

The Final Departure

Yudhishthira had no more questions. His heart had finally found some succour. Bhishma was also tired. He closed his eyes and lay still on his bed of arrows for a while. All the others stood there patiently, ingesting the wisdom shared in the past few days.

Rishi Veda Vyāsa broke the silence. He could see Bhishma needed rest. He also saw that Yudhishthira was ready to take the responsibility of Hastināpur. To Bhishma, he said, 'I believe Yudhishthira has found the answers he was looking for. Please allow the Pāndavas and the rest to take your leave.'

Bhishma agreed. He smiled at Yudhishthira and gave his parting message, 'May your mind be at peace O King. May you conduct many yagnas and make large charities. May you keep the gods and ancestors satisfied with your conduct. Keep your citizens happy and your ministers and officers comforted. Be the dependable one for your friends and kinsmen. And once Uttarāyana begins, when the sun moves towards the north, come to see me.'

Yudhishthira took his advice and everyone left for Hastināpur barring a few rishis who chose to stay with Bhishma.

Once back in Hastināpur, Yudhishthira was crowned the king and he resumed his kingly duties. There was a lot to do. Innumerable families had lost their men in the war. His priority was to comfort them and help them settle into their lives. But he didn't lose sight of the time. After about fifty days, as Uttarāyana began, Yudhishthira, along with everyone else in the family, returned to Kurukshetra to meet Bhishma one last time. They knew it was time for him to shed his mortal body. They carried with them all that would be needed to offer appropriate last rites to the grand old Kaurava.

Yudhishthira approached Bhishma with folded hands and greeted him. Bhishma slowly opened his eyes and held Yudhishthira's hand in his. 'I am very glad you have come here with everyone at the apt time of Uttarāyana. I feel like I have been lying on these sharp arrows for a hundred years,' he said smilingly, in spite of the exhaustion and pain conspicuous in his voice and on his face.

Bhishma then turned to Dhritarāshtra and said with a lot of compassion, 'Your sons were greedy and unrighteous. They have been given the justice they deserved. Do not grieve for them. On the other hand, Yudhishthira is noble-hearted and genuinely committed to you. He respects you like a father. Treat Yudhishthira as your own son and be aligned with him.'

Lastly, he addressed Krishna. His face shone as he venerated Krishna with glowing words and sought his permission to give up his mortal body. Krishna assented.

Bhishma then closed his eyes. He employed techniques of yoga and breath control, slowly accepting death, letting the ātmā rise upwards, out of his body.

One of the greatest of the Kuru descendants had chosen the time of his death and departed. Life had never been easy for him. Difficult choices had filled his life since his younger days. He never swerved from what he believed was his swadharma—unquestioning loyalty to the throne of Hastināpur. He had tried his best to avert the war. But when it was imminent, he chose the losing side. He could not give up his loyalty to the throne of Hastināpur.

Bhishma's commitment to Hastināpur became his fetters. He chose it even when it conflicted with the very basis of Dharma. He knew what the outcome of the war was going to be. He witnessed the total annihilation of the Kauravas without an iota of surprise or shock. Nonetheless, he was mentally at peace. He had lived an exemplary life. He was going to die on the battlefield as a warrior par excellence. And he knew the righteous side had rightly won. His beloved Hastināpur was in the most deserving hands.

Such statesmen are born but rarely in history. That is why Krishna asked Yudhishthira to gain whatever he could from the wisdom and experience of Bhishma.

In life and in death, what Bhishma never lost was poise and dignity!

ॐ

Part 2

Nārada Muni's Advice on Administration

The Pāndavas, along with Kunti, had escaped the Lākshagraha conspiracy hatched by Duryodhana and his coterie. They came out of hiding only after their marriage with Draupadi. With Drupad, Draupadi's father and the king of Pānchāla as their ally, the Pāndavas were now a force to reckon with. On the advice of the elders in Hastināpur, Dhritarāshtra agreed to divide the kingdom—Hastināpur was kept for Duryodhana and the barren land of Khāndavaprastha, flanked by the Khāndava forest, was given to Yudhishthira. Through their blood and sweat, Pāndavas converted Khāndavaprastha to the prosperous Indraprastha. In their endeavour, they were also ably assisted by Maya dānava, who was allowed to escape the burning Khāndava forest by Arjuna and save his life.

This Maya dānava was a quintessential architect. He constructed for Yudhishthira one of the most beautiful and exquisite assembly halls. Some say it was better than Indra's Amrāvati. Many princes and kings often came by to admire the assembly hall and to pay their respects to Yudhishthira, so did many rishis, to shower their blessings. One day, Nārada muni paid a visit to Yudhishthira at Indraprastha. The eldest son of Kunti welcomed the muni with utmost respect and offered him a seat.

The visits of rishis are never without a purpose. Devarshi Nārada too had a noble motivation for the visit—to impart the wisdom of Rāja dharma to Yudhishthira.[1] The technique he employed for it was rhetoric questioning—he asked questions to convey his instructions and teachings.

Nārada muni enquired:

Are you suitably engaged in activities that lead to wealth creation? Does your mind rejoice in abiding by Dharma? Do you experience happiness and comfort in life and are not given to anxiety and frustration?

Is your conduct towards your citizens chivalrous and aligned with the interest and well-being of your kingdom, like that of your great ancestors?

I hope you are not neglecting the cause of Dharma or associated practices for the cause of artha (wealth), nor are you squandering away wealth and obstructing wealth creation by overindulgence in religious practices, nor are you injuring both Dharma and artha by excessive indulgence in kāma—pleasure and lust. Are you dividing your time efficiently and appropriately to engage in all three—Dharma, artha and kāma?'

The Right Balance

In this context, Dharma has a more mundane implication and relates to the form of practices and rituals. Artha indicates activities of wealth generation and kāma, activities of pleasure. Our rishis understood the importance as well as utility of all three—Dharma, artha, kāma—for a grihastha (householder). Nonetheless, moderation was always recommended because overindulgence in one at the cost of the others would lead to an imbalance in life.

Shri Rāma gave the same advice of striking a balance among the three to Bharata when the latter met him in Chitrakoota.[2]

Our rishis have also given guidance on the division of the day for engaging in activities related to all of them. They recommend that a person should engage in Dharma related activities in the purvāhana—early part of the day, artha related activities in the middle part of the day and kāma related activities in the last part of the day.[3]

Nārada muni then enquires about Yudhishthira's preparedness in handling his ministers, enemies and affairs of the State. He asked:

> Do you examine and assess the strengths and flaws of the fourteen important possessions of yours and your enemy's by way of the seven strategies, putting to use the six attributes essential for a king?
>
> *The fourteen possessions of the king—kingdom (territory), forts, chariots, horses, elephants, armed forces, ministers and officers, royal palace, food supply, population, scriptures being followed, accounts of income and expenditure, wealth and means of sustenance.*
>
> *The seven strategies to be employed—the usual four, that is, sāma–dāna–danda–bheda, and additional three—mantra (incantations), aushadha (medicine) and indrajāla (magic).*
>
> *The six attributes*[4] *essential for a king—eloquence in speech, resoluteness, logical reasoning, memory of the past, vision for the future and understanding of policy and polity.*

Periodically assessing your strengths and weaknesses and that of the others and then striking alliances with those more powerful than you, do you focus on the activities for wealth creation to fill your treasury?

Activities of wealth creation—agriculture, trade, infrastructure (forts, roads, bridges, etc.), taming elephants, mining, taxation and establishing new settlements.

Have you ensured that the seven elements of your kingdom have not been won over by the enemy, nor have they been afflicted by addictions and indulgence due to opulence and are loyal to you?

Seven elements could mean the Saptāngas—the king, ministers, treasury, army, allies, provinces and capital city; or they could mean the seven important officers—chief of forts, commander of armed forces, chief judge, general of the army, chief priest, chief physician and chief astrologer.

Have you appointed as your ministers, people who are experienced, honest and noble, capable of understanding nuances of messages and conversations, loyal and brave? A king's success depends on good counsel.

Do you ensure that the deliberations and decisions you make are not leaked before you desire by enemy's spies disguised as your confidantes, your ministers or by yourself? I hope your State is secured by such ministers who know how to keep deliberations confidential and ensure that the State is not being harmed by the enemies.

Are you aware of the intentions of your friends, enemies and those neutral towards you? Do you act towards them as the situation demands—entering peace negotiations, declaring war or staying put, waiting for the right opportunity?

Do you employ only those who are loyal, incorruptible, trustworthy and experienced in their jobs?

Have you appointed teachers who are wise, well-learned in all scriptures and experts in their field of study to impart suitable education to the princes and the chief warriors in your kingdom?

Do you choose in your service one wise person over a thousand fools? The right guidance from even one learned person can prove beneficial in times of trouble. Even one minister endowed with intelligence, wit and courage can help the king achieve immense gains by way of right counsel.

Do the ministers justly administer your kingdom? I hope you don't agitate and oppress the citizens with unwarranted and severe punishments.

Are your royal priests well-learned in all the Vedas, capable of shāstrārtha, humble in nature, of noble birth and bereft of jealousy? Do you respect and generously patronise them?

Do you identify beneficial projects and undertake those which could yield great benefits at relatively lesser efforts, without delay and ensure these works are carried on unhindered?

Do you know the farmers and other people who work in your service? Have you ensured they are not afraid to approach you when in need?

Do you ensure people learn about your projects only when they are complete or nearing completion and not before that?

Have you appointed people to projects and positions depending on their skills and capabilities—the best in the most important ones and ones with lower skills in low-skilled jobs? I hope you have not appointed in your service those who are greedy, have a tendency to steal, are inimical to you or are too young and immature.

Is your chief of army intelligent, passionate, enthusiastic, courageous, resolute, noble and loyal to you? Are the heads of various units of the army conversant with all forms of warfare, honest and brave? Do you grant them favours and honour them?

Do you pay salaries and bonuses to your soldiers appropriately and on time, without delay? Soldiers do not remain loyal to a king who doesn't pay salaries on time and delays payments often. Anger of the soldiers can become a cause of great harm for the king.

Are your ministers and officers committed and loyal to you? Would they willingly sacrifice even their lives for you in a war?

Have you ensured there is no officer in your service who frequently violates your directions, imposes his own will on the people and teams he works with and seeks to manipulate resources according to his desires and whims?

Do those whose performance exceed expectations get compensated according to the work they have done? Do they get recognition for their service by you?

Do you take care of the families, wives and children of those soldiers, officers and employees in your service who give up their lives for your sake?

Do you honour and patronise people of wisdom and virtue?

Are all your forts well equipped with reserves of wealth, grains, water, weapons and also with capable archers and artisans?

Through your spies, do you always keep a close eye on the activities of your enemies without their overt knowledge?

Seeing your enemy weakened by problems, do you assess the capabilities of his counsel, army, resources and passion and lead an attack to subjugate him quickly, if he is weaker and vulnerable than you?

Do you seek to win over the enemy's army commanders to your side by enticing them with riches?

Before attacking the enemy outright, do you first seek to leverage the strategies of sāma–dāna–danda–bheda to get the enemy to surrender?

Do you ensure that your kingdom is well fortified and equipped to resist any attack before attacking the enemy? Having attacked, do you show exemplary courage and valour on the battlefield to defeat the enemy? Having won over the enemy, do you make sufficient provisions to protect the territory won?

Do you fight in the war wholeheartedly with the desire to defeat the enemy without making any concession for the seasons of reaping or famine?

Do you have officers and agents spread over your and enemy territory to achieve tasks beneficial to your kingdom and to protect your kingdom?

I hope the weak enemies earlier subdued by you are not raising their heads against you, strengthened by their army, smart counsel and allies.

Have you employed only extremely trustworthy people to attend to your personal tasks such as cooking your food, helping with your robes, manning your rooms and protecting you closely? I hope you have brave bodyguards in your service who are committed to protect you from any danger.

I hope your helpers do not make propositions to tempt you to indulge in gambling, drinking, women and other such activities and extravagances during the working hours of the day.

Are your expenditures lower than your income; is your expenditure either one-fourth, one-half or three-fourth of your income, not more?

Do your bookkeepers and accountants present to you daily accounts of income and expenditure of the kingdom in the early part of the day?

Do you spend money for the welfare of elders, teachers, traders, artisans and others in your kingdom who are in need?

Do you take care that the interests of the citizens are not harmed due to the menace of thieves, greedy officers, whims of princes and women of the royal household?

Are the farmers of your kingdom happy and not wanting in seeds and grains? Have you built many large reservoirs in your kingdom so that the farmers don't have to depend only on rainwater for agriculture? Are you providing them loans at minimal interest when they need them?

Are the honest people of your kingdom gainfully engaged in various trades and business-related activities? Trade and business are pivotal to the prosperity of the kingdom.

For the protection of the cities, are the villages as well equipped as the towns, and the outskirts as well equipped as the villages? Are these areas completely under your administration?

Do you have a police force actively moving around in the cities and villages, including places that are difficult to access, to apprehend thieves and dacoits?

Do you take care of the women of your kingdom? Are they secure and well-protected?

On hearing news that requires urgent attention, I hope you do not continue to enjoy the comforts of your royal chambers; just thinking about the matter is not enough.

Are you earnest and just, like Yama, the lord of Dharma, while punishing offenders? Are you humble and generous towards those who are learned and venerable? Do you evaluate both those whom you like and those you don't before carrying out any dealings with them?

Do you ensure that your citizens are happy with you and do not join hands to conspire and rebel against you and are not enticed by the enemy with bribes to revolt against you?

Are your ministers, especially those dispensing justice, fair and incorruptible? I hope they do not falsely accuse honest people and unjustly seize their wealth out of greed or ignorance, or punish the innocent harshly hoping to extract more wealth. Likewise, I hope they do not let an offender get away with impunity even after being caught red-handed taking bribes.

Do your ministers and judges adjudicate without bias when there is a dispute between a rich person and a poor person, without succumbing to the greed of wealth or influence of the rich?

Do traders from all over come to your kingdom to trade their wares? Are these traders well respected by your officers? Do your officers collect designated tax from these traders without trying to extract more by presenting a wrong picture?

Do you provide adequate resources as tools to all kinds of artisans to carry on their work unhindered at least for four months[5] at a time?

Have you made provisions to protect the State from not just enemies but also fire, snakes, wild animals, diseases and so on?

Do you look after those who are differently abled, orphans and ascetics, as a father looks after his children?

Do you know about the exemplary tasks, which are in the interest of the kingdom, achieved by the people? Do you duly and publicly acknowledge and commend their efforts?

Having talked about the affairs of the State and about managing enemies, Devarshi Nārada advised Yudhishthira on the importance of leading a disciplined life, continuing to learn from the experts and taking care of his own self. He said:

Have you, first and foremost, attempted to win over all your senses before desiring to subjugate the enemy?

Do you wake up before sunrise and don't give in to untimely sleep? Do you deliberate on matters of importance before the sun rises? Then having taken a bath and dressing up, do you meet with your council of ministers to deliberate on issues and provide an audience to people who have come to seek your favours? I hope you do not ignore citizens who come to you with their grievances.

Do you keep your body free of illness by eating healthy food, consuming the right medicinal herbs and practising discipline (through exercise and fasting)? Do you keep your mind free of agitation and at peace by serving the elders and the wise and seeking their company?

Are the vaidyas (doctors) in your service conversant in अष्टांग चिकित्सा (eight kinds of treatment) and are they your well-wishers and committed to your well-being?

Eight kinds of treatment—kāya chikitsā (internal medicine), bāla chikitsā (paediatrics), bhoot vidyā/graha chikitsā (psychiatry), shalya chikitsā (surgery), urdhvānga/shālākya (ophthalmology), agad tanra (toxicology), rasāyana/jarā chikitsā (geriatrics), vrishya/vājikarana (sexology/aphrodisiacs).

Do you remain steadfast in the Dharma that was practised by your ancestors, which is the root of the Vedas? Do you act in accordance with the principles of Dharma?

Do you propitiate the gods through various yagna and offer charities according to the scriptures?

Do you periodically seek guidance from those who have significant experience as well as an understanding of the science of administration and those who have deep knowledge of scriptures?

Do you continue to regularly study the sciences of warfare, weaponry, chariots, horse and elephant keeping and manoeuvring, social sciences, administration, adjudication, non-overt measures of subverting the enemy (incantations, poison, etc.)?

Do you remain watchful of not succumbing to the fourteen vices that have the potential to destroy the kings?

The fourteen vices are—gratification of the five senses, planning alone regarding the affairs of the kingdom, consultation with people who are not proficient, failure to implement decisions, inability to keep the counsel secret, opening many battlefronts at once, omission of auspicious practices, not believing in the wisdom of the Vedas, not keeping the company of the wise, falsehood, anger, inattention, procrastination and indolence.

I hope your presence doesn't agitate or excite passions in people around you and there are always people with you carrying auspicious symbols and articles.

I hope your intellect and your behaviour are aligned with all that I have just expounded to you. Such intellect and action will bring you long life, success and fame.

With this, Nārada ended his exhortation. Yudhishthira, grateful for his advice, bowed to the muni and promised to adhere to the guidance provided by him.

This episode about Nārada muni appears in the Sabhā Parva of Gitā Press's Mahābhārata, but not in the critical edition compiled by Bhandarkar Oriental Research Institute (BORI). I have included some interesting points from the episode here.

This style of teaching via rhetoric questioning is seen in other texts too. One prominent example is the dialogue between Shri Rāma and Bharata in

Ayodhyā Kānda, sarga 100, where Shri Rāma imparts guidance on administration and policy matters to Bharata. In fact, there is a lot of similarity between the discourse of Shri Rāma and Bharata and this one between Nārada and Yudhishthira, with some verses being the same in the two dialogues.

On one hand, it could mean that this episode is an interpolation in the Mahābhārata as deduced by the work of BORI, but on the other, it also indicates how the principles enunciated remained relevant in times of Rāmāyana, the Mahābhārata and even today.

ॐ

Part 3

Vidura Niti: Lessons on Life and Living from Vidura

Dhritarāshtra's Anxiety

Born to Rishi Veda Vyāsa and a handmaiden of Ambikā, Vidura was the stepbrother of Dhritarāshtra and Pāndu. He was appointed as the prime minister of Hastināpur when Pāndu was crowned as the king. He continued as the prime minister even after Pāndu, struck by misfortune, relinquished the throne and Dhritarāshtra took over as the king.

Vidura's loyalty to Hastināpur and to Dhritarāshtra was unfailing and so was his adherence to Dharma. He always stood up for what he believed was right and didn't mince words while sharing his opinion frankly with the king. He always gave thorough and thoughtful advice which was in Dhritarāshtra's long-term interest even if that wasn't what Dhritarāshtra wanted to hear. At times, Vidura's honesty and forthrightness irritated Dhritarāshtra, especially when all he wished to hear was a validation of his actions.

Vidura had suggested to Dhritarāshtra to give up his eldest son Duryodhana soon after his birth. The nimmitas[1] accompanying his birth sounded a death knell for the family, he had concluded. 'O King, you have ninety-nine other sons. Sacrifice this one son and save the family,' Vidura had advised. Dhritarāshtra did not listen to him. To be fair to Dhritarāshtra, he did not have any inkling of the scale of disaster his son was destined to bring.

When the travesty of a game of dice was being played in the Hastināpur assembly, Vidura and

Vikarna were the only two who spoke against the deceit of Shakuni and Duryodhana. Vidura warned of the dire consequences for the entire family if the game was allowed to continue. His words were proven correct just a few years later.

After the Pāndavas lost the second game and accepted thirteen years of exile, Dhritarāshtra was worried about the backlash from the citizens. He knew his sons were in the wrong. The Pāndavas were unfairly treated and duped of their kingdom and dignity. Dhritarāshtra called Vidura to discuss how to assuage the anger of the people. But instead of suggesting some smart and shallow tactics, Vidura, as was in his nature, recommended undoing the injustice meted out to the Pāndavas by asking them to return and giving Indraprastha back to them. His advice made the blind king furious.

'What you are suggesting is in the interest of Pāndu's sons—what about mine? I expected you to give me unbiased advice but here you are making a case in favour of the Pāndavas,' Dhritarāshtra shouted. In the bout of anger, he even asked Vidura to leave. Vidura did that. He went to spend a few days with the Pāndavas who, at that time, were living in the forest just outside the city. But once his anger cooled down, Dhritarāshtra realised his folly and asked Sanjaya to bring Vidura back home. For Dhritarāshtra, Vidura was more than a prime minister of Hastināpur; he was his friend and his well-wisher, someone he could count on to give the most suitable and correct advice.

Though the king didn't always follow Vidura's recommendations, especially when they conflicted with Duryodhana's desires, having Vidura to talk to was a comfort he cherished. His overindulgence of his son stopped him from taking correct decisions even when he knew what was right. But that didn't stop Vidura from being true to his king, to Hastināpur and to his own self. Taking the decision was the king's prerogative, giving the right advice was his responsibility. He never compromised on his Dharma till the very end.

That is why, even after Kauravas lost the war and Pāndavas won, Yudhishthira requested Vidura to continue as the prime minister of Hastināpur, a role Vidura fulfilled with utmost commitment. And when Dhritarāshtra decided it was time to leave the kingdom and spend his last years in the forest, Vidura gave up his position and home and followed Dhritarāshtra to the forest where he eventually gave up his body.

While Vidura was always objective and spoke from a position of wisdom, there was one profound conversation between him and Dhritarāshtra that deserves a special mention. This conversation took place when, after their successful completion of exile, the negotiations with the Pāndavas were going on about Indraprastha. Sanjaya had returned from Upāplavya with the message that the Pāndavas were ready for both war and peace, but they were not ready to tolerate injustice any longer. Sanjaya was yet to share the message. He intended to do that the next morning. But his demeanour that evening, when he came to inform the king about his arrival, had left Dhritarāshtra distraught.

Dhritarāshtra had sensed that war was unavoidable. He had no delusions about the outcome even though he kept hoping against hope for his son's victory. His mental agitation did not let him sleep at night and he lay awake. He knew there was only one person he wished to talk to. He called for Vidura and Vidura came immediately.

What followed was a conversation that has been recorded in history as *Vidura Niti*—the policy of Vidura. This episode appears as a sub-section within Udyoga Parva known as Prajāgara Parva, which literally means 'Sleepless/Lying awake'.[2]

Vidura came as soon as he learnt that the king wished to see him. It wasn't too often that the king called so late in the night, hence Vidura knew it must be something important. He entered the king's chamber to find Dhritarāshtra looking visibly disturbed.

Dhritarāshtra wasted no time in expressing his anguish. 'Sanjaya has returned from Upāplavya. He came to see me and blamed me for the situation we are in. But he didn't share what Yudhishthira said. He said he will convey Yudhishthira's message in the court tomorrow morning. The suspense is stressing me out. I am not able to sleep. You are the only one I trust to tell me honestly what is good for me. Tell me what you think.'

Vidura understood the king's distress. He responded in his trademark style—straightforward and honest, 'Four kinds of people tend to lose their sleep at night—one who has got into a dispute with someone way more powerful than himself, one who has lost everything he had, one who is overcome by lust and a thief looking to steal at night when others are asleep. Are any of these a cause of your concern? Is it the greed for someone else's wealth that is burning you?'

Dhritarāshtra ignored Vidura's allusion. Nor did he take offence to it. Instead, he said, 'Vidura, there is no one in our family whose wisdom is as rooted in Dharma as yours. Hence, I wish to hear from you some words of wisdom for my sake.' He asked Vidura to talk to him about topics that could bring some peace to his mind. In reply, Vidura spoke about a range of subjects related to value systems and ethics, personal qualities, traits of a good leader and king and many others.

Vidura's objectivity, practicality, common sense and deep understanding of the human psyche shine through in his exhortations.

ॐ

Of Ones, Twos, Threes and More

To soothe the king's heart, Vidura shared his learnings and honest observations about the human psyche, desirable and undesirable character traits in people and the need for understanding them, both for self-introspection and improvement, and to smartly deal with all kinds of people. More importantly, Vidura wished to use this occasion to coax the king into doing the right thing. He began his address by exhaustively listing out the characteristics of the wise and the unwise:

- A wise person (pandit) is one who:[3]
  - Knows and does what is worth doing and refrains from actions that shouldn't be done
  - Has shraddhā[4] in the divine power beyond self
  - Is not tainted by anger, joy, pride, stubbornness and ego
  - Does not boast prematurely of his achievements—people get to know of his work only after it is accomplished but never know what is in his mind
  - Does not let heat or cold, wealth or the lack of it, fear or joy, interfere with the work he has set out to do
  - Knows his potential and takes up tasks accordingly, without looking down upon any task, however small
  - Engages in a task not from a position of his desire but from a position of responsibility and the requirement of the task
  - Deliberates upon and plans his actions properly before starting a task, and once started, he stays

disciplined, doesn't procrastinate and sees it to completion
- Doesn't chase after things he cannot get, doesn't grieve over something that is destroyed and does not become stupefied when faced with calamity
- Doesn't get overexcited when praised nor becomes agitated when criticised; he stays calm in every situation
- Is articulate and eloquent in speech, manifests strong logic and reasoning in thought and speech and is able to grasp the essence of any talk or book quickly
- Remains humble even after achieving great wealth, education or position.

✦ A foolish person (muudha) is one who:[5]
  - Is proud without any learning
  - Has luxurious needs despite his poverty
  - Wants to acquire wealth without hard work
  - Disregards his own duties but rushes to fulfil the responsibilities of others
  - Desires those who disregard him, disregards those who care for him
  - Picks up unnecessary fights with those much stronger than him
  - Unnecessarily doubts everyone and everything
  - Wastes time in doing things which can be quickly completed and spreads himself thin by getting involved in many tasks at a time
  - Blames others for his faults
  - Gets angry over others doing tasks even though he is incapable of doing them himself
  - Gives unnecessary advice to the underserving—one who cannot or would not understand—and seeks refuge with a miser.

After discussing the qualities of wise and unwise, Vidura used a very distinct style of narration. He followed a numerical sequence in listing out observations as well as some dos and don'ts as ones, twos and so on.[6]

- One who, while being wealthy enough to eat good food and wear expensive clothes, doesn't look after the well-being of those who work for him and deserve to be nourished by him is indeed cruel.[7]
- One person may commit a pāpa (e.g., a crime like stealing) and many others may enjoy its result. The repercussions, however, are borne only by the doer and not those who partook the spoils.[8]
  This dictum aligns with a popular story of the dacoit who looted people for his livelihood. He used to rationalise his actions, thinking he was doing all the pāpa for the welfare of his family. Once Nārada told him to ask his family if they would be willing to share his pāpa, just like they shared the wealth he stole for them. He was shocked to hear his family refuse to be his partner in sharing the pāpa. The incident made him lose interest in the ways of the world. He transformed himself and became a sage, performing many austerities.
- One may or may not be killed by an archer's arrow, but when hit by the intellect of a wise person wronged, the king and the entire kingdom would be destroyed.[9]
- Poison can kill only a person who drinks it,
  Weapon can kill only a person who is hit,
  But one undesired leak from the office of the administrator can destroy the entire kingdom along with the king.[10]
- Do not eat a tasty feast alone,
  Make no important decision alone,

Do not walk on an isolated path alone,
Stay up not, when everyone else is asleep, alone.[11]

- There is only one way to cross a sea—using a boat. There is only one way to get to heaven—adherence to Truth.[12]
  Here Truth must be understood as Dharma. It doesn't imply rigid insistence on spoken truth but that which is in the interest of the sustainability and growth of the larger society, as explained by Bhishma earlier.
- There is one major disadvantage to people who are forgiving—their forbearance is often misunderstood as their weakness. The capacity to forgive is a strength. It is a virtue of the powerless and an ornate jewel of the powerful.[13]
- Dharma alone is beneficent.
  Forbearance alone is the best approach to establishing peace.
  Wisdom alone leads to contentment.
  Non-violence (in thought, speech and action) alone can bring lasting happiness.[14]
- Two types of people are destroyed just like the creatures living in pit holes gobbled up by a snake:[15]
  - Scholars who do not travel
  - Kings who do not fight wars.

  This is an interesting dictum which encourages travel, quite contrary to overseas travel being considered a taboo in some communities in medieval Bhāratvarsha.
- Two ways of wasting wealth acquired through genuine means:[16]
  - Giving to the undeserving
  - Not giving to the deserving.
- Two actions that get a person respect and adoration:[17]
  - Avoiding harsh speech

- Not honouring the wicked.

✦ Two tendencies that suck the blood out of a person like sharp thorns:[18]
  - Desire that the person cannot afford
  - Anger that cannot achieve its purpose.

✦ Two kinds of people who are led by the views of others:[19]
  - A person who desires the opposite sex only because other people find them desirable
  - A person who venerates someone only because people around him are doing so.

In contemporary terms, these are people who are easily vulnerable to peer pressure.

✦ Two types of people do not deserve to live:[20]
  - A rich person who doesn't do any charity work
  - A poor person who cannot bear physical inconvenience.

✦ Two kinds of people who are elevated even beyond the heavens:[21]
  - The powerful who choose to forgive
  - The poor person who is charitable.

The Greater Dāna

Heeding the advice of Krishna and Veda Vyāsa, Yudhishthira undertook the Ashvamedha Yagna after being crowned the king of Hastināpur. The yagna saw participation from almost all the great rishis of the time as well as the royal families from across Bhāratvarsha. Guests from all communities came from far and wide. There was no dearth of delicacies to serve the guests. Ghee and butter were in abundance, so were sweets. Yudhishthira had opened his treasures for charity.

Announcements made round the clock said, 'दीयतां भुज्यतां चेष्टम्—May people be given whatever they seek. May people be fed whatever they like.' The guests as well as the citizens of Hastināpur couldn't stop praising the generosity of the Pāndavas.

One afternoon, after the yagna was completed and the guests sat relishing the feasts, they heard a loud roar as if lightning had struck. Everyone was astonished to find the source of the roar—a weird-looking mongoose with blue eyes and a body that was half golden. When the mongoose had the attention of the people around, it spoke in a human voice, astonishing everyone even more. 'This grand Ashvamedha Yagna is no match in merit to the dāna given by that Brāhmin who lived near Kurukshetra and survived on उञ्छवृत्ति[22] (eating only gleaned food grains from the fields).'

These words of the mongoose came as a shock to everyone. They encircled the mongoose and asked rather sternly, 'Who are you? You seem to be an imposter in this gathering of learned people. What do you know about charity, scriptures and merits to even make a comparison disparaging this magnificent yagna of our king?'

The mongoose responded humbly but firmly:

> I wish no offence. I am only saying what I have seen and experienced. Let me tell you about that poor Brāhmin of Kurukshetra and the mystery of my half-golden body.
>
> Those were the days of hardship. Famine had struck this land. Food was in shortage. Fields had dried. In such a situation, imagine

the plight of this Brāhmin of Kurukshetra and his family consisting of his wife, son and a daughter-in-law who ate only food grains gleaned from farms. For days together, the family had to go hungry because they couldn't find any grains.

Then one day, the older Brāhmin got a kilo[23] of barley. He came home and asked his wife to cook it for dinner. Having done their pujā and having made their offering to the Devatās, the family sat down to eat. Just then a man came to their door, seeking food. 'A guest is next to God,' said the elder Brāhmin and without an iota of regret happily offered his share of the food to the guest. The man was very hungry. He quickly gobbled down the food and asked for more. This time the Brāhmin's wife offered her share to him. The man ate that too but wasn't satisfied.

The son then offered his share, which was also eaten by the guest. The daughter-in-law then offered her food to him, without complaining. She knew that as a host it was her responsibility to ensure the guest was satisfied. Finally, the man said he was full and happy and left.

At that time, I was roaming around that Brāhmin's home searching for food. I noticed that a grain of barley had fallen on the floor of their kitchen. I went to get that grain. But as soon as I touched it, half of my body transformed into gold. This miracle was possible only due to the merit earned by the family due to their large-heartedness even in times of adversity. I saw a chariot of the Devas come to carry the family to heaven.

Since that day, I have been visiting various yagnas, hoping to find one as meritorious as that Brāhmin's dāna so that the other half of my body also turns into gold. That was the reason for my coming to this yagna. I tried to rub my body multiple times on the grains spilled here, but unfortunately, I will have to go back disappointed. That is why I said that this Ashvamedha Yagna of Yudhishthira is of no match in merit to the dāna of that Brāhmin family.

The people gathered there heard this story of the mongoose, speechless. A very important lesson was conveyed by the mongoose about the merit of charity—it is good that a person gives charity when capable of doing so, like Yudhishthira was, but great indeed is the person who gives to a seeker when he himself survives on the barest minimum, harbouring no malice or regret.

The greatness principle stated by mongoose aligns with the dictum mentioned by Vidura to Dhritarāshtra about one of the two kinds of people who are elevated beyond the heavens. This story is mentioned in the Ashvamedhikā Parva of the Mahābhārata.

- Three levels of capabilities exist in people—high, medium, low. Depending on their level, they should be assigned to work, in accordance with their capabilities.[24]

- Three offences that bring great fear and harm to reputation:[25]
  - Theft of other's wealth
  - Desiring/Violating others' wives
  - Abandoning one's well-wishers and friends.
- Three tendencies that are destructive to self and open doors to hell; these must be given up:[26]
  - Lust
  - Anger
  - Greed.
- Four types of people to be avoided from any secret discussions and dealings—those who are:[27]
  - Foolish
  - Reckless
  - Procrastinators
  - Needless flatterers.
- Four things give instant results:[28]
  - The will of the gods
  - The influence of the wise
  - The humility of the learned
  - The destruction of the unrighteous.

  Krishna tells Arjuna in Srimad Bhagavad Geetā, 'I take birth in every yuga when Adharma rises for 'परित्राणाय साधूनां विनाशाय च दुष्कृताम्—*Protect the noble and destroy the wicked.' Many times, to establish Dharma, protection is not enough; punishing and destroying those who are causing Adharma is critical to achieving the result.*
- Five categories of people one is sure to encounter wherever one goes:[29]
  - Friends
  - Enemies
  - Neutrals
  - Dependents who seek shelter

– Those who provide shelter.

- Five senses of perception (indriyas) in humans are—eyes (sight), ears (sound), nose (smell), skin (touch) and tongue (taste). If any hole (flaw) develops in even one of them, intelligence drains out like a stream of water from the hole of a pot (*and leads to flawed decision-making*).[30]

Avadhoota and His Teachers

In Srimad Bhāgavatam, there is a story of an avadhoota—an ascetic who has achieved liberation from all bondages of life. In the story, the avadhoota talks about how he gained wisdom from his twenty-four teachers. His teachers included living beings as well as inanimate objects around him, observing which he learnt precious lessons of life. While the entire story is worth reading, here I will mention only five of the teachers. The avadhoota's learnings from them corroborate Vidura's observation about how a flaw in even one indriya can lead to a person's downfall.

The avadhoota says he learnt the need to control the senses from the downfall of the following five.

1. Fish: A fish is baited with food because of its vulnerability to taste.
2. Elephant: An elephant is trapped using a she-elephant exploiting its need for touch.
3. Moth: A moth meets its death flying into fire attracted to it by its sight.
4. Deer: A deer is caught by attracting it with the sound of a hunter's flute.
5. Bee: A bee is killed by getting trapped into a lotus attracted to its smell.

There is a subhāshita about this phenomenon:

कुरङ्गमातङ्गपतङ्गभृङ्ग-मीनाः हताः पञ्चभिरेव पञ्च ।
एकः प्रमादी स कथन्न हन्यते, यः सेव्यते पञ्चभिरेव पञ्च ॥

A deer, elephant, moth, bee and fish are killed because of their vulnerability to one of their senses. What then to say about those (humans) who are enslaved to all the five senses?

Hence, the incessant insistence of indriya nigraha in all the discourses and scriptures.

- Six vices to be kept at bay by one who seeks prosperity and success:[31]
  - Sleep
  - Drowsiness
  - Fear
  - Anger
  - Lethargy
  - Procrastination.
- Six virtues worth imbibing and never giving up:[32]
  - Truth
  - Generosity
  - Enterprise
  - Absence of jealousy
  - Forgiveness
  - Fortitude.
- Six things that bring comfort in life:[33]
  - Wealth
  - Good health
  - A spouse who is favourably inclined
  - (A spouse) who is soft in speech

- Obedient children
- Professional acumen.

- Six enemies (षड् रिपु) that reside in the mind, which if reined in, prevent a person's downfall:[34]
  - Lust
  - Anger
  - Greed
  - Attachment
  - Lethargy
  - Jealousy.
- Six professionals that depend on these six kinds of people for their living:[35]
  - Thieves on incautious people
  - Doctors on the diseased and unwell
  - Prostitutes on lustful men
  - Priests on householders
  - Kings and administrators on people in discord
  - Intellectuals on the ignorant.
- Six situations that make life joyful:[36]
  - Being healthy
  - Being able to earn according to one's capabilities and inclinations
  - Being debt-free
  - Engaging with decent people
  - Not having to live in a foreign land
  - Living fearlessly.

  Living in a foreign land was considered as a hardship in ancient times, unlike now. A similar observation is shared even by Yudhishthira in Yaksha Prashna. It could probably be because travelling itself was an arduous task, without aeroplanes or vehicles, like we have today. It could also be inferred that the prosperity and climate of the Indian civilisation was more desirable as compared to others in those days. We have many accounts of visitors who came here to study and trade and also of invaders who eventually made India their home.

- Six kinds of persons are always unhappy, those who are always:[37]
  - Jealous
  - Hateful
  - Angry
  - Discontented
  - Suspicious
  - Dependent on others for their livelihood.
- Six kinds of people who should be given up:[38]
  - A teacher who doesn't give the right lessons
  - A purohita who doesn't chant mantras
  - A king incapable of protecting his people
  - A spouse who is always bitter
  - A cowherd who desires to only stay in the village
  - A barber who wishes to live in forests.
- Seven vices worth giving up by a king or a leader:[39]
  - Lustfulness
  - Gambling
  - Hunting
  - Drinking alcohol
  - Using harsh speech
  - Giving extreme punishments
  - Wasting or using resources improperly.
- Eight types of pleasures that define the essence of happiness and are attainable only in this world:[40]
  - Acquisition of great wealth
  - Embrace of our child
  - Meeting with friends
  - Lovemaking
  - Being able to talk to dear ones at the right time
  - Progress of our people

- Getting what we desire
- Respect and recognition in the society.

✦ Eight qualities that make a person illustrious:[41]
- Wisdom
- Nobility
- Self-restraint
- Deep knowledge
- Valour
- Measured speech
- Charity as per capability
- Sense of gratitude.

✦ Wise indeed is the person who understands that the essence of this body—a house with nine doors, three pillars and five observers—is that it is an abode of the ātmā:[42]

Nine doors: Two ears, two eyes, two nostrils, one mouth, one urethra and one anus.

Three pillars: The three gunas of prakriti that make the physical and mental structure of the person—sattva, rajas and tamas.

Five observers (sākshi): The five senses of perception—sight, smell, hearing, touch and taste.

✦ Ten states in which a person would not know what is right and what is not:[43]
- Intoxicated
- Inattentive
- Insane
- Exhausted
- Angry
- Very hungry
- Hasty
- Greedy
- Fearful
- Overcome with lust.

Numerical Coding

A unique encoding style is sometimes used in Sanskrit poetry for the sake of brevity and metre. For example, in one of the injunctions that Vidura quotes to Dhritarāshtra, instead of describing a list of 'things', only their number is mentioned. The meaning of the numbers is understood from the context of the verse and the colloquial usage of the terms.

एकया द्वे विनिश्चित्य त्रींश्चतुर्भिर्वशे कुरु ।
पञ्च जित्वा विदित्वा षट्सप्त हित्वा सुखी भव ।।[44]

The translation and meaning of this is:

Deliberating on two (action or inaction according to the call of duty), using one (intellectual faculty), three (enemy, ally and neutral) should be brought under control using the four (strategies of sāma–dāna–danda–bheda), having first won over five (senses of perception—sound/ear, sight/eye, smell/nose, touch/skin, taste/tongue), and then undertaking either of the six (approaches of dealing with opponents—sandhi, vigraha, āsana, yāna, samshraya, dwaidhi bhava) giving up the seven (vices of lustfulness, gambling, hunting, drinking alcohol, using harsh words, giving severe punishments and wasting available resources).

The explanation of the numbers in the verse varies in different commentaries, but the gist is largely similar. The interpretation given here is from Gitā Press's Mahābhārata, Volume 3 (Sanskrit–Hindi).

Another example of such a usage can be found in the Rudra Chamakam section of Sri Rudram, a Vedic mantra dedicated to Lord Shiva. In the Chamakam, various material desires are requested from Shiva by the devotees. The 11th anuvāka (chapter) of the Chamakam enumerates a set of odd and even numbers, which the devotee wishes should be favourable to him. A sample of the verse is:

एका च मेतिस्रश्च मेपञ्च च मेसप्त च मे नव च म एकदश च मे..

Let these be granted/favourable to me. One, three, five, seven, nine ...

The odd numbers asked are from 1 to 33, and even numbers from 4 to 48 in multiples of four.

According to some commentaries,[45] these numbers indicate groups of things such as:

1 means nature/prakriti,

3 means the three gunas, namely sattva, rajas and tamas,

5 means the pancha mahābhutas—earth, water, fire, wind and space,

7 means the five sense organs plus the mind and the intellect,

9 means the nine openings in the human body.

ॐ

Prahlāda's Discourse on Qualities of a Leader

The night progressed and so did Vidura's and Dhritarāshtra's conversation. Vidura shared an episode from history, a dialogue between Prahlāda, the noble king of the Asuras and a rishi's son named Sundhavā.[46]

Prahlāda explained to Sundhavā what makes a good leader:

- People regard, trust and follow the words and actions of the king who:
  - Makes decisions without being driven by lust or anger
  - Recognises and patronises the deserving (artisans, artists, people of learning, etc.)
  - Has expertise in administration and polity
  - Is conversant with the wisdom of the scriptures
  - Discharges his duties with responsibility and promptness.
- Prosperity comes to the king who:
  - Invokes trust in his citizens and allies
  - Punishes only after a crime has been indisputably proven
  - Knows when to punish, how much to punish and when to forgive.
- Only that person is considered steadfast in wisdom who:
  - Does not discount a weak enemy
  - Engages with the enemy with discretion and intelligence, while always being on guard
  - Does not get into unwarranted fights with the more powerful
  - Does not shy away from showing his valour on the battlefield when the time demands it.

- A person who has the following traits is sure to subjugate his enemies:
  - Resilience: Doesn't become discouraged by challenges and troubles and doesn't give up
  - Perseverance: Gets up after a fall and continues to work hard towards the fulfilment of his goals.
- Happy is the person who keeps away from:
  - Futile travel in a foreign land, away from family
  - Hobnobbing with the wicked
  - Desiring women other than his wives
  - Hypocrisy
  - Stealing
  - Alcohol
  - Backbiting and maligning others.
- A person is said to be wise who:
  - Doesn't start any work out of arrogance
  - Speaks the truth when asked
  - Doesn't get into unnecessary fights even for the sake of friends
  - Doesn't lose his cool even if slighted.
- Such a person gets praised everywhere who:
  - Doesn't hold malice towards anyone and is kind to all
  - Doesn't provide surety for an accused while being poor himself (*doesn't get into disputes with others when he is himself weak*)
  - Doesn't speak with arrogance
  - Forgives a quarrel (*doesn't hold on to a fight and grudge, lets it go*).
- Such a person is loved by all who:
  - Doesn't put up a haughty demeanour
  - Doesn't boast of his valour before others
  - Doesn't use hard words against others even when agitated.

- A person is considered respectable and of noble conduct who:
  - Doesn't stoke old hostilities which have subsided with time
  - Doesn't behave with arrogance nor with over-humility
  - Doesn't use his distress as a licence to commit unrighteous deeds.
- A person is considered of good conduct who:
  - Doesn't go into raptures about his own happiness
  - Doesn't take pleasure in the grief of others
  - Doesn't repent after having given to charity.
- A person who learns and understands practices, traditions, behaviours, languages and the history of people in different places, and also what they consider good and bad, is sure to win over the people wherever he goes.
- Gods bestow prosperity on the person who gives charity, conducts scripturally ordained rites, rituals and ceremonies, worships the gods and engages in auspicious activities.
- No harm comes to a person who:
  - Eats little and only after sharing with all in his care
  - Sleeps little even after a long day's work
  - Gives charity/help even to his enemy when sought by the latter.

Having shared the teachings of Prahlāda to Sundhavā, Vidura coaxed Dhritarāshtra to accept the Pāndavas and give them what was rightfully theirs. This was not only the right action, but also a wise thing to do in the interest of the Kauravas and Hastināpur. 'The sons of

Pāndu have always revered and obeyed you. They are like five Indras in their skills and splendour. Call them back and give them their kingdom. If you do that, neither the gods nor the people will put any blame on you,' he said.

ॐ

Tips on Practical Living and Character Building

Dhritarāshtra heard Vidura's words patiently, but his mind was still agitated and bewildered. He lacked the will to act on what Vidura was proposing, but he was keen to hear more. 'Tell me what is in the interest of both Yudhishthira and the Kauravas. My mind is not at peace, hence I am seeing bad omens everywhere,' he said.

Vidura had not minced words to tell Dhritarāshtra what the best recourse for his agitated mind was. The king's unwillingness to act wasn't lost on him.

He spoke with an added emphasis:

शुभं वा यदि वा पापं द्वेष्यं वा यदि वा प्रियम् ।
अपृष्टस्तस्य तद्ब्रूयाद्यस्य नेच्छेत्पराभवम् ।।

It behoves one who is a well-wisher to tell the one whom he cares for all that is in the latter's interest—be it good, bad, pleasant or unpleasant, even if not asked.

Hence, whatever I say is only what is in your interest and beneficial to the Kauravas. Do listen to me with attention. Do not let unrighteous tasks achieved by dishonest means allure your mind, nor should you let apparent setbacks from well-intentioned tasks through righteous means discourage you.[47]

Vidura shared further pearls of wisdom:

On Attitude and Approach to Decision-Making and Work

- A wise person should decide only after deep deliberation, not in a hurry or on impulse. Factors to deliberate upon:[48]
  - Objective of the project
  - Expected outcome
  - Activities that will have to be undertaken to achieve the outcome
  - Potential consequences of those activities
  - Potential gains for self (the doer): *What is in it for me?*[49]
- A person must act only after having considered the potential consequences, pros and cons of both scenarios—doing the task as well as not doing it. Some tasks are just not worth doing because even if done, the hard work will be futile because the results will not be worthwhile.[50]
- Smart people do not delay or cause hindrances in tasks which have the potential to produce great benefit with little effort.[51]

  Act on low-hanging fruits with alacrity.
- A person who plucks unripe fruit from trees gets no rasa and destroys the seed, but one who waits for the fruit to ripen gets both the rasa and the seed.[52]

  Timing matters, so does patience.
- It is important to have a sense of fear from:[53]
  - Doing what should not be done (that is, which is socially or ethically unacceptable)
  - Ignoring that which must be done
  - Leaking confidential information before the task is achieved
  - Consuming intoxicants.

- Wealth gets generated by auspicious deeds,
  Increases by determination and wisdom,
  Becomes stable by consistent skill and enterprise,
  And is preserved through self-control and discipline.[54]
- Do unto others as they do unto you. Good conduct should be reciprocated with good conduct and deception with deception.[55]
- A person who has the following traits has no worry about the destruction of a source of livelihood:[56]
  - Energy
  - Intelligence
  - Ability to create impact
  - Spirit of perseverance
  - Industriousness.
- The mantra to achieve success in all that a person does is twofold:
  - Do whatever is for the benefit of all and brings joy to yourself
  - Having taken up a task, perform it with the attitude of surrendering the results to God.[57]
- A person who, reflecting on the sane advice given by wise people, undertakes an action after thinking thoroughly about its consequences attains lasting glory. Even the most outstanding advice given by most skilled people is of no use if it is not understood well, or even if understood, is not implemented well. [58]

  An advice's worth is only in its action.
- A person should not consider doing an act which seems to confer profits in the short term but leads to major losses in the long term. You should certainly consider doing an act which seems to produce short-term losses but which will bring

significant benefits in the future. A loss is not a loss that leads to eventual progress. But a benefit which eventually causes heavy damages should necessarily be considered a loss.[59]

- A person who knows remedies to ward off calamities before they strike, is resolute in his endeavours undertaken in the present and is aware of what work is left to be done or is pending from the past is never deprived of material wealth.[60]
- Whatever is done repeatedly by way of action, speech and thought attracts the doer towards itself. Hence, you should always engage in actions that are beneficial and usher in well-being.[61]
- Perseverance is the root of prosperity, gains and favourable results. A person who is spiritedly perseverant and doesn't give up achieves happiness and greatness in stature.[62]
- An individual is indeed a person of courage who, after having suffered a major material setback, doesn't give up but with firm resolve strives to gain back what was lost, using the right policy.[63]
- Qualities that act as fuel to enhance wealth and prosperity:[64]
  - Resoluteness
  - Tranquillity of mind
  - Self-control
  - Purity in speech, body and mind
  - Compassion
  - Softness in speech
  - Non-betrayal of allies.
- Qualities essential for achieving growth and progress:[65]
  - Enterprise

- Self-control
- Skills
- Caution
- Patience
- Good memory
- Beginning a task only after a thorough analysis of all the relevant aspects.

✦ An intelligent person who keeps away from petty quarrels that fools engage in achieves fame in the society and avoids unwarranted misery.[66]

✦ Win over anger by forgiveness,
Win over the wicked by goodness,
Win over a miser by generosity,
Win over falsehood by truth.[67]

✦ Anything said at an inappropriate time, even if right, even if said by the teacher of Devas, Brihaspati himself, will attract disregard and humiliation of the speaker's intellect.[68]
Timing is everything.

✦ Conduct yourself during the day in such a way that you can have a peaceful sleep at night. Live the eight months of a year in such a way that the four months of monsoon (four months of break) can be happily sustained. Live life as a youth in such a way that you can have a comfortable old age. Live your life in such a way that life after death becomes happy.[69]
Four months of monsoons were considered as the 'rest and recuperation' period in the past. During these four months, no agricultural activity or army marches were undertaken. That was the reason Shri Rāma waited for four months to start the search expedition for Seetā after Sugriva was crowned the king.

- Let go of a person (a family member) if that can protect the family at large. Let go of the family if that will protect the village. Let go of the village if that will protect the nation. But for the sake of the ātmā, let go of the world itself if you must.[70] *Vidura had conveyed this message to Dhritarāshtra at the time of Duryodhana's birth and also when all omens indicated the destruction of the family. He reminded him multiple times after that to rein in Duryodhana and protect the family, but in vain.*

On Character Traits and Consequences

- The name of the family is no testimony to character, only the person's conduct determines his character.[71]
- It is not wealth that defines nobility but good conduct and virtue. Hence, you should strive to protect your virtues. Wealth is volatile, it may come and go but virtue once destroyed, destroys the person himself.[72]
- It is impossible to hide your flaws by wealth acquired through unrighteous means. Rather, by resorting to such wrong means, flaws not known earlier become manifest.[73]
- Just like swans desert dry lakes, wealth deserts the person who is:
  - Fickle-minded
  - Doesn't serve the elders
  - Lacks self-restraint
  - Is ignorant and indecisive.

  Also, such a person does not make any permanent friends.[74]
- A person envious of other people's wealth, beauty, strength, family, well-being or good fortune

is doomed to sorrow. Jealousy is an incurable disease.[75]

- For a haughty person, education, wealth and family reputation are tools of arrogance. On the other hand, the same education, wealth and family reputation serve as tools of self-restraint for a person of wisdom.[76]

  The Sanskrit shloka that Vidura mentions has an interesting play of the words मद and दम. मद means arrogance and दम means self-restraint. And दम is मद read backwards. The shloka underscores the importance of a person's character which eventually affects the outcome of his actions. A tool is only as good as its user. The shloka is:

  विद्यामदो धनमदस्तृतीयोऽभिजनो मदः ।
  एते मदावलिप्तानामेत एव सतां दमाः ।।

- Old age destroys beauty,
  Intense desires and expectations disturb the peace of mind,
  Death takes away life,
  Righteous conduct destroys envy,
  Sensual indulgence destroys modesty,
  The company of uncivil persons destroys conduct,
  Anger destroys wealth,
  Arrogance, however, destroys everything a person has.[77]

- A troubled and painful life awaits the person who shows traits of intense envy, ruthlessness, animosity, deception and maliciousness. On the other hand, a person who harbours no envy, is prudent and engages in noble tasks is revered wherever he goes.[78]

- Anguish depletes beauty, anguish depletes strength, anguish destroys wisdom, anguish leads to all kinds of diseases and disorders. Anguish helps to make sure that you do not get what you desire; it only leads to more distress and brings joy to your enemy.[79]
- Even vultures do not eat the flesh of the dead bodies of the ungrateful ones who do not acknowledge and reciprocate the support and respect given to them by their friends and well-wishers.[80]

  The purport of the above is that an ungrateful person is the lowest of the low in terms of social acceptability and is shunned by all. To enhance the effect, Vidura says that even vultures who otherwise survive on dead flesh will not accept the flesh of such people, what to say of others!
- People whose minds are forever engaged in unworthy acts fail to see the virtues of others and notice only their flaws.[81]
- Excessive jealousy is akin to death; excessive tendency to pick arguments and fights destroys wealth.[82]
- The efforts of foolish people are futile, just like those swans trying to bend a rainbow, punch the sky or hold the rays of the sun. Foolish indeed are those who:[83]
  - Teach the underserving—those who do not have the capability or willingness to learn and understand
  - Become satisfied with small gains
  - Praise the enemy excessively
  - Seek favour from a person who should not be approached for favours
  - Boast indiscriminately

– Despite noble birth, do what should not be done
– Create enmity with a person much more powerful than them
– Preach to those who have no faith
– Desire something unattainable
– Get someone else's wife pregnant
– Speak ill about their own spouses
– Having received something, refuse to acknowledge it, pretending they do not remember
– Boast about giving after giving something to a seeker
– Strive to prove as truth something which is false.

On Indriya Nigraha

- Achieving control over the senses and mind is paramount (indriya nigraha) for a person who wishes to succeed.
- When a person is enslaved by his senses, his problems keep increasing like a waxing moon. Such a person can never win over his friends or enemies and is deserted by his own people. However, a person who first strives to win over his senses and his mind can have influence over friends and foes alike.[84]
- Even Devi Lakshmi, the goddess of wealth, indulges a person who has achieved mental and sensual control and does all his work after thorough investigation and caution.[85]
- A human body is pulled by our sense organs like a chariot is pulled by horses. Thus, like untrained and undisciplined horses can potentially kill a charioteer unable to steer them effectively, unrestrained senses can lead a person to doom.[86]

- A person enslaved by his senses often loses objectivity and makes the mistake of treating something non-beneficial as beneficial and sorrow as joy. Such a person loses it all—wealth, wives, health and even his life.[87]
- A person is his own enemy or his own friend depending on how well he achieves control over his mind and senses. A person who is able to control them is his own friend; a person who is unable to restrain his mind and senses and instead is driven by them is his own enemy.[88]
- A thing that has fallen in the sea is lost, so is advice that is unheard. Unworthy is a fire ritual (yagna) done without fire. Unworthy is a person who, even though well-versed in the scriptures, fails to achieve control over his senses.[89]
- Protect the stomach and sex organs by inculcating control,
  Protect hands and legs with the eyes,
  Protect eyes and ears with the mind,
  Protect the mind and speech by good conduct.[90]
- Life is a river whose waters are the five senses. This river is filled with crocodiles and sharks in the form of anger and desire. Navigate its currents of birth and death in the boat of fortitude and self-control.[91]

On Learning

- A person should imbibe good lessons from anywhere and anyone, be it a child or a mad person, just like gold is extracted from stones.[92]
- A person of fortitude gleans wisdom, good sayings and good actions from everywhere, just like those who subsist on gathering food grains collect their food from wherever they can.[93]

- Lack of humility, lack of desire to learn, haste and boastfulness are enemies of learning.[94]
- Seven pitfalls for students to watch out:[95]
  - Laziness
  - Lack of attention and mental confusion
  - Fickle-mindedness and restlessness
  - Tendency to gossip and engage in excessive banter
  - Mental rigidity
  - Pride
  - Lack of willingness to let go, and excessive greed.
- How can a person who desires ease and comfort acquire knowledge? How can a student desirous of learning be comfortable? A person who desires only comfort has to give up learning, and a student desirous of learning must give up comfort.[96]

  Learning requires focused efforts and perseverance. Only the person who has the willingness to consistently work hard can learn. Comfort is not for such a diligent student. This shloka from Vidura Niti is a popular Sanskrit subhāshita and appears in Chānakya Niti *as well:*

  सुखार्थिनः कुतो विद्या विद्यार्थिनः कुतः सुखम् ।
  सुखार्थी वा त्यजेत्विद्यां विद्यार्थी व त्यजेत् सुखम् ।।

- Even when endowed with sharp intelligence such as that of Brihaspati, the nuances of Dharma and artha can only be understood by the study of scriptures and serving the elderly.[97]

  Serving the elderly is an important tenet of Indian culture. All treatises on Rāja dharma have highlighted the need for vriddha sevā—serving the elderly. Āchārya

Chānakya says in Chānakya Sutra, 'Vinaya (humility) and discipline are cultivated through vriddhopasevā. It is by serving the elderly that a person attains practical wisdom.' The reason for such a dictum is self-evident. The idea is to instil patience and humility and also leverage the wisdom of the elderly which they have gained through life experiences to understand ways of the world and develop a positive perspective towards life.

On Friendship

- A burning flame of fire is a test of gold,
  Conduct is the test of a good person,
  Courage is tested when in danger,
  Patience is tested when faced with material loss,
  Friendship or enmity is tested when calamity befalls.[98]
- A person to whom one is expected to serve due to fear of their anger or doubt is not a friend. A friend is a person who can be trusted like your father. Others are only acquaintances.[99]
- Wise people make friends with other smart people only after thoroughly assessing their intelligence and getting to know them better by seeing them and listening to them multiple times.[100]
- To avoid becoming perplexed in any situation, respect and seek advice whenever in need from friends who are:[101]
  - Eminent in wisdom
  - Of great virtue
  - Distinguished in learning
  - Older in age.
- Friendship lasts long among those whose hearts are in sync with one another, who are together in secret dealings and are intellectually matched.[102]

- A wise person would avoid friendship with a person who is:[103]
  - Wicked
  - Imprudent
  - Wrathful
  - Arrogant
  - Rash
  - Unrighteous.
- Traits to look for in a friend:[104]
  - Sense of gratitude
  - Righteousness
  - Truthfulness
  - Generosity
  - Devotion towards the friend
  - Self-control
  - Understanding of boundaries
  - Tendency to stay steadfast by a friend.

On the Wicked and Wickedness

- Wicked people, when requested to join a certain task by virtuous people, consider it a validation of their character and begin considering themselves as noble, even though their reputation of wickedness precedes them.[105]

  Such is the power of assumed validation and self-ignorance.
- Wicked are those who do not possess these qualities:[106]
  - Forthrightness
  - Sense of righteousness
  - Control over anger
  - Sense of contentment
  - Self-restraint
  - Ability to say soothing words

  - Rectitude
  - Willingness to give and share.
- If caught with wicked people, even the innocent end up being punished, their only fault being that they were associated with the wicked. Hence, it is better to avoid the company of wicked people in all circumstances.[107]
- Wicked and foolish people tend to disregard people who are humble and modest. They think they are weak and powerless.

On Dharma

- Do not do to others what you wouldn't want to be done to you. In brief, this indeed is Dharma.[108]
  This is another well-known shloka which appears in the Mahābhārata in Anushāsana Parva also. The shloka is given here. In Anushāsana Parva, the only change is that in place of सङ्ग्रहेणैष, *the word* एष सङ्क्षेपतो *is used.*

न तत्परस्य संदध्यात्प्रतिकूलं यदात्मनः ।
सङ्ग्रहेणैष धर्मः स्यात्कामादन्यः प्रवर्तते ।।

- Do not give up your Dharma out of fear, greed or desire. Dharma is eternal but not happiness and sorrow. The ātmā is eternal but not this material body. Focus on the eternal not the ephemeral and be content. There is no accomplishment like contentment.[109]
- Look at all the powerful kings who ruled prosperous kingdoms but eventually succumbed to death, leaving all material riches behind. They would have carried nothing with them except their actions, both good and bad. Therefore, it is

better for a person to acquire Dharma through good deeds.[110]

- Consider this self as a river, the good deeds done by you as a sacred place of pilgrimage, truth the waters of the river, fortitude its banks and compassion its waves. A person who has done good deeds gets purified by a bath in it, for a self without greed accrues the highest merit (punya).[111]
- A person who indulges in prohibited actions (पाप—pāpa) has to face the consequences as prescribed for such actions. A person who performs righteous actions (पुण्य—punya) gets rewarded accordingly. Prohibited actions corrupt the intellect when done over and over again. Such corrupted intellect pushes the person further down the path of destruction. Likewise, acts of punya enhance the intellect when done over and over again, which in turn inspires a more righteous behaviour in the person.[112]
- Students are disciplined by the teacher, the people by their king. Those who do unrighteous acts thinking no one is watching are eventually disciplined by the lord of Death Yama himself.[113]
- A person who uses the money acquired through unrighteous means to conduct religious rituals in order to achieve merit in the world beyond doesn't get the fruits of the rituals due to the tainted wealth.[114]

The Do Nots

- Do not work for these six types of people:[115]
  - Do everything with a lot of difficulty
  - Extremely negligent
  - Always speak untruth
  - Are fickle in loyalty

- Without affection
- Overconfident, over-smart.

✦ Do not lend or borrow money from the following:[116]
- A king who is haughty and disrespectful[117]
- A person of suspicious character or a prostitute
- Government officials
- Army personnel
- Your son
- Your brother
- A young widow with kids
- A person who has been ostracised.

✦ Do not let these six kinds of people live in your home:[118]
- An idler who is unfit for any work
- A glutton
- A person who is despised by other people
- A person who is deceitful
- A person who is cruel
- A person who shows no understanding of the appropriateness of time and place in his behaviour and actions
- A person who dresses indecently.

✦ Do not seek favour, however distressed you may be, from people who are:[119]
- Excessively miserly
- Abusive in speech
- Ignorant of scriptural teachings
- Cunning
- Disregard those who are worthy or respectable
- Ruthless
- Ungrateful
- Quarrelsome.

✦ Do not ever fully trust the following:[120]
- Kings

- Powerful people
- Your enemies
- Snakes
- Lifespan
- Luxuries.

✦ Do not entertain a person who is:[121]
- Wicked
- Ungrateful
- Does not use wealth appropriately on people in his care
- Lacks a sense of shame.

✦ Some people are rich in virtue and some rich in material wealth. The wealthy who are lacking in virtue should be surely shunned.[122]

Observations on Life

✦ Strength is of five types. These are given here in ascending order of importance:[123]
- Physical strength (bodily as well as of the army)
- Good counsel that comes from the appointment of good ministers
- Wealth and resources
- Noble birth in a family of reputation
- Human intelligence. This is the greatest of all as all the other strengths can be obtained by it.

✦ Metal that is malleable doesn't have to undergo treatment by fire. Likewise, a wise person aware of his own strengths and weaknesses and that of others bows down to the more capable and powerful. He does not pick unnecessary fights and saves himself from needless suffering.[124]

✦ A poor person always eats food that is tasty. Hunger adds taste to the food. Such enjoyment is not available to the rich. Abundance and immoderation diminish the digestive power of the rich while the poor can digest even iron.[125]

- The biggest fear of ordinary people is losing their livelihood, the next biggest is the fear of death; the eminent people however fear disrepute and infamy in the society.[126]
- Nothing intoxicates like power. A person drunk on power comes back to sobriety only after a fall.[127]
- People die and others take birth,
  Societies shrink and grow,
  People seek favours and are sought favours from,
  Sometimes one gains and sometimes one faces losses,
  Sometimes there is happiness and sometimes sorrow.
  No one remains untouched by these turns of life.
  Knowing thus, a wise person neither grieves nor rejoices.[128]
- Gambling is known to create animosity amongst people. Hence, not even for fun should a person indulge in it.[129]

Chānakya calls dyuta (gambling) one of the worst addictions arising from intense kāma. Others—like alcohol addiction, lust, hunting—largely impact the person afflicted and with good counsel, the situation can be managed. But gambling can destroy entire royal families and disrupt kingdoms, as happened to King Nala and Yudhishthira. In the case of Yudhishthira, he wasn't addicted, rather he resisted the invitation at first. Nonetheless, the game led to the initial uprooting of the Pāndavas and the eventual doom of the Kauravas.

- A person without knowledge, a sexual union without progeny, people without food and a country in anarchy—these are worthy of pity.[130]
- Sleep cannot be subdued through more sleep, neither can women be won over through lust, fire can't be triumphed by fuel, nor can drinking help a person overcome alcohol addiction.[131]
  Some solutions are about 'not doing'.
- Happy is the person who has won over his friends with generous gifts, who has won over his enemies on the battlefield and who has won over his wife by taking care of her welfare and comfort.[132]
- All the wealth, food and women of this entire earth cannot satisfy the never-ending desires of even one man; a person who reflects on this doesn't get perplexed by the vagaries of life.[133]
- Women are considered highly blessed and virtuous; they illuminate the home they live in and usher in wealth and prosperity in the household. It is necessary for a man to always respect them and look after their well-being and safety.[134]
- Ten benefits that accrue to one who bathes regularly:[135]
  - Physical strength
  - Beauty and handsomeness
  - Clear voice
  - Clear complexion
  - Softness of touch
  - Fragrance in the body
  - Cleanliness
  - Radiance
  - Youthfulness
  - Attention of the opposite sex.

- Six benefits that are gained by a mitabhukta—a person who eats sparingly:[136]
  - Good health
  - Long life
  - Physical strength
  - Mental happiness
  - Healthy progeny
  - Cannot be humiliated for gluttony.
- Eight items that do not break a vrata (i.e., ritual fast or vow):[137]
  - Water
  - Root vegetables
  - Fruits
  - Milk
  - Ghee
  - Guru's instructions
  - Medicine
  - Ask or instruction of a priest.
- A person who hates others is never considered honest or intelligent. Such a person sees only virtues in tasks done by those whom he likes and only demerits in those he hates.[138]

  Judgements are rarely neutral; often they are coloured by our emotions.
- A person who is virtuous, knows the limits and propriety in social interactions and is humble and modest—irrespective of whether he is of high or low birth, he is far better than hundreds of people of high birth but lacking in these qualities.[139]
- When the gods ordain failure on a person, they do so by polluting his buddhi (intelligence) making him indulge in unworthy thoughts and activities.

> At the time of destruction, it is the buddhi that fails a person and a bad policy appears like a good policy.[140]

'O King, it appears to me that the intellect of your sons has also been corrupted due to their imminent doom. Hence, they seek enmity with the Pāndavas. You too don't seem to understand this. Yudhishthira is wise and capable of reigning a kingdom effectively and justly, way more than your own sons. Only he is fit to rule this glorious kingdom,' emphasised Vidura.[141]

The king was in no mood to act as advised, but he continued to urge Vidura to share more insights.

Vināsha Kāle Viparita Buddhi

Chānakya Niti mentions a quote which is similar to the dictum of Vidura that when failure is ordained, it happens through perversion of buddhi. The shorter version of the quote is popular and quoted often—विनाशकाले विपरीत बुद्धिः—Vināsha kāle viparita buddhi, which means 'At the time of doom, a person's intellect acts opposite to all reason'.

The entire shloka is given below. It makes the same point, giving an example from itihāsa.

न निर्मितः केन न द्रुष्टपुर्वः न श्रूयते हेममयः कुरङ्गः ।
तथाऽपि तृष्णा रघुनन्दस्य विनाशकाले विपरीत बुद्धिः ।।

Never has a golden deer been created by anyone before nor seen or heard. Even then, Shri Rāma chose to chase such a deer out of desire (to please Seetā and fulfil her wish of having the deer). This eventually led to the abduction of Seetā by Rāvana.

The Confrontation between Rishi Shakti and Rājā Kalmāshapāda

In Ādi Parva, there is the story of Rishi Shakti and King Kalmāshapāda narrated by a Gandharva named Angarparna to the Pāndavas. It is apt to be mentioned here.[142]

One day Rājā Kalmāshapāda of the Ikshvāku dynasty went on a hunting expedition all by himself. All day long he hunted wild boars and other dangerous wild animals. Extremely tired and hungry, he headed back to the city in the evening. On the way he came face to face with Shakti, a rishi himself and the eldest of the hundred sons of Maharshi Vashishtha.

The road was narrow and only one person could pass through at one time. Shakti was a Brāhmin, a rishi's son and very learned. It was a social norm to give way to the more respectworthy person in such situations. As he was a rishi, he was considerably more worthy of respect compared to even a king. Or so thought Shakti.

But Kalmāshapāda was very tired and not in the position to think straight. He expected the rishi to make way for him, for, after all, he was the king. It became a matter of pride for both to pass through first, with neither willing to relent. Hunger and fatigue were taking a toll on the king already and now this impasse frustrated him even more. He pulled out a whip and lashed at Shakti.

Shakti was furious with rage and cursed Kalmāshapāda that he would become a man-eating rākshasa. Not thinking much about it at that time, the king rode away. After some time, the curse began to slowly have its effect. A rākshasa spirit started taking grip of the king's intellect to begin with. In that state of mind, the king committed a blunder of feeding rice mixed with human flesh to a Brāhmin who had come to his palace to seek food. Angered at this insult, that sage also cursed Kalmāshapāda that he would become a man-eating rākshasa. The second curse accelerated Kalmāshapāda's transformation into a cannibal rākshasa.

Kalmāshapāda left his kingdom and started roaming around in the forest, scrounging for food. As destiny would have it, he came across Shakti once again and gobbled him up out of his anger for the curse and his hunger for human flesh. But that didn't satiate Kalmāshapāda. One by one, he ate the other ninety-nine brothers of Shakti as well.

Rishi Vashishtha was distressed to hear about the death of all his sons. His grief as a father who had lost all his sons led him to thoughts of giving up his own life. But the news of the pregnancy of his eldest son Shakti's wife reignited his will to live, if nothing else, for this child. This child of Shakti grew up and earned fame as Rishi Parāshara. Rishi Veda Vyāsa was the son of Rishi Parāshara and Satyavati.

One day, before Parāshara was born, when Rishi Vashishtha and his pregnant daughter-in-law were walking through the forest, they saw Kalmāshapāda looking for food. If the rishi had wished, he could have killed Kalmāshapāda to avenge the death of his sons. But he did not. Rishi Vashishtha took some water in his palm and sprinkled it over Kalmāshapāda, liberating him from the curse. Therein lies the greatness of Rishi Vashishtha. He was aware that

Shakti's curse was extremely severe and unreasonable, even if his anger towards Kalmāshapāda was correct.

Shakti, who was otherwise a learned rishi, met his end due to the curse he pronounced on the king in a bout of extreme anger. That Kalmāshapāda had erred is beyond doubt, but as someone expected to display a high degree of mental control, Shakti should have considered if the punishment he was going to inflict was commensurate with the king's offence. But then, as Vidura said and Chānakya agreed, vināsha kāle viparita buddhi.

It is not surprising that our scriptures focus excessively on mastering indriya nigraha—the control of our senses and our impulses of anger, lust, greed, ego, attachment and jealousy. Only when the control of the mind and senses becomes second nature can we expect our decisions and actions to be balanced and not clouded by our impulses and biases.

ॐ

The Justice of Prahlāda

To emphasise to Dhritarāshtra that being just towards the Pāndavas was his kingly duty, Vidura narrated another episode from the life of Rājā Prahlāda that showed how the highly esteemed king of the Asuras attained fame and glory by remaining fair and forthright in proclaiming a judgement even though it went against his son's desire.[143]

Once upon a time, both Virochana, the son of the much-revered Rājā Prahlāda of the Asuras, and Sundhavā, the son of Rishi Angirā, wanted to marry a girl named Kesini. Both young men were accomplished, smart and eligible. But Kesini could marry only one of them. Not wanting to take the responsibility of deciding in favour of one and facing the ire of the other, she said, 'I will marry the greater amongst the two of you. Both of you mutually decide and come back to me.'

Virochana and Sundhavā were in a fix. They couldn't decide the parameters to evaluate greatness, but each believed he was greater. Nonetheless, in this bid to determine comparative greatness, they added another clause—whoever lost out would have to give up his life.

Since they couldn't come to an agreement, they decided to find someone to adjudicate. Sundhavā suggested Prahlāda should be the judge. 'Even though he is your father, I trust the king to make a fair decision,' he said. Virochana agreed and both of them went to Prahlāda's court.

Prahlāda was surprised to see the two boys in court. He had never seen them together earlier as they were not friends. Sundhavā explained the reason for their visit and asked him to pronounce who between Virochana and him was greater and therefore suited to marry Kesini.

Prahlāda looked thoughtfully at Sundhavā and asked him in front of the entire assembly, 'What happens to the king who gives a false judgement?'

'A king who gives a false judgement is punished with defeat and capture at the hands of his enemies. If he does so to act favourably towards someone he likes, then multiple generations of his have to suffer in hell,' responded Sundhavā firmly.

'Then I must be truthful—my son has lost to you,' said Prahlāda without hesitation.

Addressing Virochana he said, 'Rishi Angirā, Sundhavā's father, is greater than me, his mother is greater than yours and Sundhavā is more accomplished than you are. He is indeed the greater one.' Then turning to Sundhavā he said, 'I have proclaimed the truth to the best of my abilities. Now my son's life is in your hands.'

Sundhavā was pleased. 'You have been honest and hence I give up claim over your son's life. He need not give up his life. I only request you to make the same proclamation in front of Kesini so that she agrees to be my wife,' he said.

Prahlāda agreed. Kesini and Sundhavā were married, and Virochana's life was saved.

Concluding the story, Vidura reiterated, 'Therefore, O King, do not push your sons towards destruction just for the sake of a piece of land and be truthful towards the Pāndavas. Do remember, the Devatās do not guard us the way the cowherds guard their cattle with a stick. Instead, when the Devatās desire our well-being, they inspire our intellect with reason and wisdom, leading us towards making decisions that are beneficial to us. There is no doubt that the person who is just and focused on the well-being of all will achieve all that he desires.'

ॐ

Advice for a King

Over the course of the dialogue, Vidura shared many dictums specifically applicable to kings, administrators and leaders. Some interesting ones have been collated here.

- A king who desires to obtain and maintain his kingdom must know the state, measure, periodic gain and loss of the following aspects of his kingdom:
  - Treasury
  - Territory and people
  - Army and judiciary (danda).[144]
- A king ignorant of the above cannot retain his kingdom for too long. But one who regularly deliberates on the above and is well-versed with the different aspects of Dharma and artha is able to obtain and maintain his kingdom.[145]
- A kingdom acquired as an inheritance is soon lost if the king is not conversant with policy and administration.
- A king who thinks 'now I have obtained the kingdom' and becomes ignorant and immodest loses his prosperity just like old age depletes beauty.[146]
- The king should act proactively and passionately to protect the borders of his kingdom and strive to destroy his enemies.[147]
- People are satisfied with a king who constantly works to keep his people happy in every way—with his eyes, speech, mind and actions. But the king who provides no pleasure and only induces fear in his people eventually gets overthrown by the same people.[148]

With eyes: The way he looks at his people.
With speech: The way he talks to them.
With mind: The way he constantly thinks about their welfare when making any decision.
With action: The way he conducts his actions for their well-being.

- It is not an assembly which has no elders. They are not worthy elders who do not speak in accordance with Dharma. It is not Dharma which is bereft of satya. It is not satya which is corrupted by deceit.[149]
- It is easy to find people who are always ready to flatter and say whatever is agreeable to the listener. Rare is a speaker who is willing to speak what is not agreeable to the listener but is beneficial for him. Equally rare is a listener who can take such feedback. To the king, the employee of assistance is one who takes recourse in Dharma and without worrying about whether the king will like it or not, says only what is in the interest of the king.[150]
  The first shloka about this is very well known and often quoted Sanskrit subhāshita. It appears in both the Mahābhārata and Rāmāyana. In the Mahābhārata it is spoken by Vidura to Dhritarāshtra and in Rāmāyana by Māricha to Rāvana. The shloka in Sanskrit is:

  सुलभाः पुरुषा राजन्, सततं प्रियवादिनः ।
  अप्रियस्य तु पथ्यस्य, वक्ता श्रोता च दुर्लभः ।।

- A king should hire workers and officers according to their suitability for the job. After clarifying their roles and responsibilities, the wages and allowances commensurate with the State's income and expenditure should be agreed and fixed. It is through capable staff that the king can accomplish even the most difficult of tasks.

- The king (employer) should never stop or confiscate the rightful payment of the employees still in service. Even the most loyal workers and ministers, when deprived of their livelihood, are likely to desert the master and ally with the opponents.
  Manpower turnover and poaching by competitors were as much of an issue then as now. The more times change, the more they remain the same!
- To inspire trust and confidence in his employees and officers, it is important that the employer does not overtly express his anger towards people who have been loyal and devoted to him. These committed workers are the ones most likely to stand by their master in times of distress.
- The king should readily acknowledge the contributions of the committed workers who, knowing the master's intentions, discharge their duties with honesty and dedication and who advise only what is in the interest of the master. The king should confer the same honours and favours to such workers as he would to his own kinsmen.
- A worker who does not respect the word of the master, refuses to do the work assigned to him, uses unacceptable speech and is arrogant should be immediately expelled.[151]
- Only a person who has learnt to control both anger and joy deserves to rule a kingdom. Such a person does not get deluded and remains steadfast even in calamities.[152]

- Generating wealth needs help from allies and it takes wealth to get allies. One cannot be achieved without the other.[153]
- Eight qualities to look for while appointing an ambassador:[154]
  - Unassuming
  - Not given to cowardice
  - Shows alacrity in action
  - Compassionate
  - Honest and incorruptible
  - Healthy
  - Belongs to a reputed family
  - Elegant in speech.
- The king should not talk about any work being done related to Dharma, artha and kāma until it is completed. Let the action do the talking. Never let the intentions be known and never let the royal decisions/discussions leak out.[155]
- A king who can maintain the confidentiality of his counsels both externally and internally and keeps a watch on all and everything through his spies is likely to enjoy prosperity for a long time.[156]
- Such a person should never be involved in confidential discussions:
  - Who is not an ally
  - Who is an ally but not learned
  - Who is learned but does not have control over his mind and senses.[157]
- Never appoint ministers and officers without thorough assessment because the king's finances and the counsel he receives depend on these ministers and officers.[158]
- The following should never be made witnesses:[159]
  - Palmists

- Corrupt businessmen
- Gamblers
- Doctors
- Enemy of the accused
- Friend of the accused
- Artists and performers.

This is to avoid conflict of interest, both in favour and against the accused. Even today, doctors are mainly used as expert witnesses in courts of law and not witnesses for or against the accused. As for palmists, gamblers and such, the idea seems to be to avoid as witnesses people who can be easily influenced or whose testimony cannot be cross-verified.

- ✦ A king well versed in the application of the sixfold policy of protecting his kingdom—sandhi (peace), vigraha (war), āsana (neutrality), yāna (marching), samāshraya (alliance) and dvaidhibhāva (waging war with one and making peace with another), is watchful of the consequences of his actions—increase, decrease or status quo (of wealth, territory, people, goodwill, etc.), knows his own self well and is respected by all successfully reigns over the earth.[160]
- ✦ A king whose expressions of anger and joy are impactful towards achieving desirable consequences, who himself supervises critical activities of the State and has the treasury in his control reigns over the earth.[161]
- ✦ An enemy worthy of being eliminated should not be set free when captured. If the enemy is stronger than yourself, then you may also politely attend to him. But as soon as he gains enough strength, the enemy should be killed, because if not killed, he

will soon pose a dangerous threat to your life and kingdom.[162]

- People do not desire a ruler whose grace is fruitless, and anger serves no purpose. Just like women do not desire an impotent husband.[163]
- A king who is without deceit and is capable, enterprising, grateful, intelligent and upright succeeds in getting supporters, friends and allies even when his treasury is empty.[164]
- Six are the doors through which counsel leaks. Therefore, to protect one's wealth and well-being, a king should not only be vigilant but also strive to keep these doors shut. In that way, he can continue to do productive work and keep his enemies in check.[165] These six doors are:
  - Intoxication
  - Sleep
  - Ignoring important information/lack of attention to spies
  - Trust in wicked ministers
  - Flaws in one's own self (traits such as anger, lust, lack of control in speech, etc.)
  - Incapable spies/envoys.
- Never let your guard down, even if you are far away, after having instigated animosity with a person capable of inflicting great harm on you.[166] This advice should be followed when dealing with very intelligent people too. The arms of such people are long enough to harm anyone, however far he may be located, when harassed.[167]
- Avoid aspiring for an acquisition which involves extreme exertion or transgression of propriety or necessitates you to bow down to the enemy.[168]

- Do not express your disagreement in a discussion with a king who is in the company of wicked counsellors. Do not even say things like 'I am not convinced'. Instead, make a good excuse and leave.[169]

ॐ

Death and Immortality

Dhritarāshtra posed another question, 'Vedas tell us that human beings have been given a hundred-year lifespan. But why is it that most people do not live their full lifespan?'

Vidura answered:

> There are six traits that, like sharp swords, cut the life of a human. These are:
> - Extreme self-pride
> - Excessive talking
> - Unwillingness to let go
> - Excessive anger
> - Extreme self-centredness
> - Betraying one's kin.[170]

Earlier, trying to convince Dhritarāshtra to do the right thing, Vidura had shared with him an approach to immortality. He said, 'Amongst bathing in holy teerthas and being forthright, forthrightness[171] is considered as more distinguished. You too must resort to forthrightness and behave equitably towards both the Pāndavas and Kauravas. Such behaviour will bring you fame and glory. As long as a person's glory is remembered on this earth, he enjoys the pleasures in the heavens.'[172]

यावत्कीर्तिर्मनुष्यस्य पुण्या लोकेषु गीयते ।
तावत्स पुरुषव्याघ्र स्वर्गलोके महीयते ।।

Immortality of Indradyuman

The same teaching was conveyed to Yudhishthira by Rishi Mārkandeya during the vanvās of the Pāndavas. The rishi had narrated a story of King Indradyumna in relation to immortality and a place in heaven.[173]

Yudhishthira played host to many tapasvis and rishis during the twelve years of their vanvās. The Vana Parva of the Mahābhārata has documented many conversations which the Pāndavas had with the visiting rishis.

Once Rishi Mārkandeya came to see them in the forest. Amongst other things, Yudhishthira asked the rishi if there was any being alive at that time who was older than the rishi. In response, Rishi Mārkandeya narrated to him a fascinating story of Rājā Indradyumna.

> Once there lived a king by the name of Indradyumna in Bhāratvarsha. He was a just king and hence much loved by his subjects. Given his good deeds, he attained swarga after his death. He lived a life of peace and comfort in swarga for many years until one day it was conveyed to him that his time there was over, and he would have to go to earth again and take birth there.
>
> Indradyumna was not happy and enquired the reason for this. 'Your glory is remembered no more on earth. This indicates that you have lived your time in heaven and now you must return to earth,' he was told.

Not the one to give up, Indradyumna wished to check for himself if it really was the case that no one remembered him on earth. He descended to earth and approached Rishi Mārkandeya.

'Do you know me?' he asked the rishi.

'We don't spend more than a night in any place and are constantly travelling on pilgrimages. We are always busy undertaking various austerities. So we do not always remember people even if we have met them earlier,' Rishi Mārkandeya answered.

'Hmm, is there anyone you know who is alive and older than you?' he asked the rishi.

After some thought Rishi Mārkandeya replied, 'I know of this owl that lives in the Himālayas. He is older than I am.'

Indradyumna took the form of a horse, asked Rishi Mārkandeya to sit on his back and took the rishi to the Himālayas to find the owl. On meeting the owl, the king asked again.

'Do you know me?'

The owl thought hard and said he did not remember him.

'Is there anyone you know who is alive and older than you?' asked Indradyumna.

'There is a heron who lives in the lake named Indradyumna. He was born much before me. He would probably know you,' answered the owl.

Together, all three of them went in search of the heron.

The heron too didn't remember Rājā Indradyumna. He directed them to a turtle living in the same pond who was older than him.

On meeting the turtle, they all asked together, 'Do you know this King Indradyumna?'

The old turtle squinted his eyes and took a good look at the king. He paused for a bit and suddenly his eyes moistened and his face took an expression of intense joy. He spoke with his heart full of happy emotion.

He said, 'Oh yes, of course, how will I not know him? He is the great Rājā Indradyumna. During his reign, he conducted many yagnas and gave away a lot of charity. He donated thousands of cows. This lake in which I live was formed due to the constant droving of the cows which were gifted by him, creating a depression on the land.'

As soon as the turtle spoke these words, a chariot emerged from the heaven to carry Indradyumna back. Indradyumna asked the chariot to wait till he dropped the owl and the rishi back to the place where he had met them. He proceeded to heaven in the chariot only after that.

Rishi Mārkandeya ended the narration after reciting a few shlokas to bring home the message of the story.

दिवं स्पृशति भूमिं च शब्दः पुण्यस्य कर्मणः ।
यावत्स शब्दो भवति तावत्पुरुष उच्यते ।।

As long as the memories of the good deeds of a person remain in this world and the world beyond, until then he is known to exist and reside in the heavens.

अकीर्तिः कीर्त्यते यस्य लोके भूतस्य कस्यचित् ।
पतत्येवाधमाँल्लोकान्यावच्छब्दः स कीर्त्यते ।।

As long as the ill-fame of the bad deeds done by a person is remembered in this world, he is known to fall and reside in the lower regions (hell).

तस्मात्कल्याणवृत्तः स्यादत्यन्ताय नरो भुवि ।।
विहाय वृत्तं पापिष्ठं धर्ममेवाभिसंश्रयेत् ।।२३।।

Therefore, seeking refuge in Dharma, one must engage in only virtuous actions that bring merit and give up indulgence in actions that lead to harm.

ॐ

Finding Mental Peace

Dhritarāshtra, still anxious, expressed his insecurity to Vidura, 'I haven't been fair to Yudhishthira. Therefore, he will certainly destroy my sons in the war. This thought continues to agitate my mind. Tell me something which will help me find peace.' Vidura gave some profound tips to Dhritarāshtra.

- ✦ The way to find peace from mental agony and anguish is by:
  - Gaining knowledge
  - Cultivating discipline in thought and action
  - Achieving control over the senses
  - Overcoming one's greed.
- ✦ Through wisdom, a person can overcome his fears,
  Through discipline and doing austerities, a person can achieve greatness,
  By serving the teachers, a person can gain knowledge,
  By practising Yoga, a person eventually achieves mental peace.
- ✦ A person attains happiness through proper study, just war, righteous actions and disciplined life.
  But those persons who are disunited with their own tribe, intending to hurt others through unrighteous action, cannot get a good night's sleep even when in possession of a comfortable bed and in the company of their spouses. Such people find no peace, no glory. They do not like candid advice even if it is in their interest and refuse to see what is good for them as if headed towards their own destruction.

Vidura used the opportunity to drive the importance of being united with the Pāndavas into Dhritarāshtra's mind and said:

> A tree standing alone, however strong, is easily uprooted by a storm, but when standing together as a group in a forest, it can resist even the strongest of storms. Likewise, a person without allies standing alone is easily overpowered by his enemies but not when his kinsmen stand strongly along with him. Together they flourish. The Pāndavas are your sons too and have suffered a lot. Call them back and take care of them. Let your sons and the Pāndavas protect each other so that your enemies cannot take advantage of your disunity.[174]

Dhritarāshtra was happy to hear everything worthy of being heard and he was hungry for more. But nothing—no advice, no prodding—could move him into action to prevent the impending war. Even after such a long discourse, Dhritarāshtra's response was that come what may, he was incapable of giving up Duryodhana. He was aware that if a war took place, victory would adorn only the one aligned to Dharma.[175]

Much later, he did try to speak to Duryodhana to discourage him from fighting an outright war with his cousins. But by then it was too late. In the war that followed, not only did Dhritarāshtra lose Duryodhana, but also his other ninety-nine sons and all his grandsons as well.

Nonetheless, gratitude is due to Dhritarāshtra for making this conversation take place. This conversation continues to shine the light of wisdom on us even today.

ॐ

Part 4

Kāma Geetā: The Song of Kāma

Uttarāyana, the sun's movement towards the north, had started. Bhishma was waiting for this time to let go of his battered body and embrace death. He was given all the honours that he deserved and a very respectable cremation by Yudhishthira, joined by all the Pāndavas as well as Dhritarāshtra, Vyāsa muni and Krishna, amongst others.

Yudhishthira had collected himself a little after the extreme grief of losing his near and dear ones in the war, with the long discussions he had with Bhishma. But having completed the last rites of his dear Pitāmaha, he was once again overcome with intense guilt and sorrow.

This time though, Vyāsa muni wasn't amused. 'Your intellect is not cleansed of your kāma and hence you are not able to think objectively. Because you are not able to rid yourself of a strong attachment to things, you are still disillusioned about the war and the outcome, despite all our attempts to explain to you that what happened was the demand of the situation. But you do not have faith in our words. Your intellect keeps harping on the loss of your near and dear ones like a child who cannot let go of a toy. It was your Dharma to fight the war and you know it well. A king who understands his Dharma doesn't give in to mental agitation like you are doing. Pull yourself out of it, live your Rāja dharma and fulfil your responsibilities towards your people,' he said and advised Yudhishthira to conduct an Ashvamedha Yagna.[1] He also explained how Yudhishthira could collect the resources for the yagna.

Krishna attempted, once again, to help Yudhishthira see the root cause of his recurring agony and suggested an approach to deal with it. He said:

> I will be straightforward with you because only honesty redeems, deceit is akin to death. You haven't yet fulfilled your responsibilities, nor have you won over your enemies. The enemies are not outside but inside you. Do you not know them?[2]
>
> There are two types of diseases that humans suffer—physical and mental. Both of them are mutually related. One doesn't exist without the other. Physical health is determined by an equilibrium of kapha, vāta and pitta in the body, and mental health by sattva, rajas and tamas. When any one of these factors increases or reduces, health suffers. The three restrain one another and keep the balance intact.
>
> Our happiness is reined in by sorrow and sorrow is stabilised by happiness. Some people deal with their grief by thinking about their joyful days. Some people remember the days of pain and sorrow when life was happy and good. That keeps them grounded. But you don't seem to remember your grief from the past. Or is it your nature that you just switch off from the past?
>
> You keep lamenting over the war and the death of your cousins and others, but you don't remember how Draupadi, your wife, who was menstruating and dressed in just one piece of garment, was dragged and humiliated in the Hastināpur court by the same people you are lamenting for.
>
> You don't remember how unjustly your kingdom was snatched and you were exiled to the forest. You don't remember the hardships of the forest, nor the

outrageous attempts of Jayadratha and Keechaka to violate Draupadi.

A war like the one with Dronāchārya and Bhishma faces you even today. The enemy challenging you is your own mind. You are the only warrior who can rein in that mind. No allies can come to your aid, no weapons will be of any help in this war. You must fight it alone, all by yourself. And if you lose this war against your mind, we can only imagine what situation will befall all of us. If you ponder over my statement deeply, you will know what your purpose and responsibilities should be from now on. Also remember that birth and death are a of part life and administer your kingdom justly, like your ancestors.[3]

True renunciation doesn't come by just giving up material or bodily pleasures. It is futile to talk about renunciation if the mind continues to dwell upon worldly attachments. This two-syllabled word 'मम' (this is mine) leads to intense attachment and indulgence in worldly objects and is the cause of all bondage, while this three-syllabled word 'नमम' (not mine) instils a sense of detachment from worldly objects and is the key to eternal bliss.[4]

Who and what can cause harm to someone who, even after winning the rulership of the whole world and all material pleasures, doesn't get too attached to them, always aware that these riches are not mine (न मम)? But the person who, even after having outwardly renounced worldly objects, accepting to stay in the forest and subsist on roots and fruits, doesn't stop desiring those material pleasures continues to suffer. Such a person is as good as dead.

Therefore, identify this enemy, that is, attachment, which is within you. Recognise that this attachment is deluding you and leading you astray from your Dharma. Do not let yourself get carried away by emotion. Redeem yourself from the great pain and fear it has inflicted on you.

Kāma (desire/attachment) is the root cause of all actions. But people of wisdom know that unchecked kāma is also the root cause of pain and suffering. They encourage freeing oneself from the bondage of kāma. Many yogis have vanquished their desires by resorting to the path of yoga. Whatever activities they undertake, be it the study of scriptures, various austerities, yagna and donations, they do them without any desire for personal gain. Controlling the mind and desires is pivotal to Dharma.

I will share with you a story narrated by persons of learning and wisdom. It is called the Kāma Geetā—The Song of Kāma. In that, Kāma speaks of its prowess and its defiant resilience of clinging to the human mind in one form or another.

The Kāma Geetā

Those who attempt to subjugate me using the strength of their weapons, I arise in that very strength of theirs as arrogance.

Those who attempt to subjugate me by undertaking various yagnas and giving large donations, I grow again in their heart as desire and pride like consciousness involutes in things that move.

Those who attempt to subdue me with studying the Vedas and the related texts, I reappear in them like the Divine manifests in the physical bodies.

Those who try to vanquish me with their patience and courage, I camouflage and appear in their emotions and thoughts unknown to them.

Those who subdue me by undertaking severe tapasyā, I reemerge in their tapasyā in the form of their ego and ambition.

Those who wish to destroy me by taking recourse in achieving moksha, make me laugh. They are already bound to me by their very desire for moksha.

I am the only one invincible in this world.

Yudhishthira, ruminate on what I have told you. Free your mind of unwarranted attachment and guilt towards your relatives who were killed in the war and resume your responsibilities as the king of Hastināpur.[5]

Kāma, a Sanskrit term, is a very profound idea encompassing but not limited to desires, attachments, lust, sensual and material pleasures, ego, arrogance, greed, ambition, obsessions and so on. The words 'kāma, desires, attachments' used here should be understood as all of these traits. Attachment also includes attachment to worldly relationships and attachment to कर्ता भाव (doership), not just objects of sensual pleasure.

Kāma is one of the purushārthas prescribed for Hindus. Indic view understands well that desires and attachments are important for progress to take place and for people to connect with one another. However, it is also understood that unending desires, attachments and unwillingness to let go cause pain and suffering. These are the same tendencies which lead to conflicts and wars by colouring our intellect and hindering objective thinking; they divide the society into 'us versus them'.

One very intriguing trait of kāma which is beautifully expressed in the Kāma Geetā is that even efforts meant to control kāma end up creating more kāma. We have seen this repeatedly in life as well as in stories in our scriptures. Severe tapasyā, scriptural learning, rituals and donations often enhance obsession, ambition as well as pride unless there is a constant introspection that leads to acute awareness of self and of any rising negative traits. All the powerful Asuras in our Purānas had done intense tapasyā, controlling their senses to achieve great boons. Eventually, these boons became their nemesis because they sparked severe arrogance and ego in them, leading to their downfall.

One of the ways of remaining humble in success and hopeful in failures is to give up attachment to कर्ता भाव (kartā bhāva)—the sense of doership. That is why Krishna tells Arjuna on the battlefield of Kurukshetra that he should fight not with a sense of ego but consider himself as just an instrument of divine will—निमित्तमात्र (nimitta mātra).

Developing such an attitude is by no means easy, as seen in Kāma's narration. It is important to know the utility of kāma in human life while emphatically and empathetically checking its excesses in ourselves through the practice of any of the different paths of yoga that help develop objective self-awareness, to begin with.

This discourse of Krishna to Yudhishthira is yet another instance of our scriptures emphasising the need and importance of indriya nigraha, a topic covered in detail in the previous chapters.

ॐ

Part 5

Vyādha Geetā: The Sermon of a Meat-Seller

Among the many interesting stories narrated by Rishi Mārkandeya to Yudhishthira and the Pāndavas during their stay in the forest, one such discourse deserves a special mention. This is the story of a young Brāhmin receiving lessons in the nuances of Dharma from quite unlikely teachers.

A Lady Shows the Way

Once there lived a Brāhmin named Kaushika. He was well known for his deep study of the Vedas along with all six Vedāngas[1] and the austerities he performed. One day, as he was sitting under a tree and studying, a bird defecated on his head. Furious, he cursed death upon the bird. In no time, the bird fell dead before him. His anger subsided on seeing the bird lying lifeless on the ground and guilt gripped his heart. 'What have I done? Engulfed with anger, I took an innocent life,' he lamented. With the thought of the bird still in his mind, he went to get bhikshā[2] for his food in the village nearby.

He approached a house where he had received bhikshā before. The door was open. He called out loudly, 'Bhavati bhikshām dehi—O lady, give me bhikshā.'

The lady of the house was washing dishes when she heard Kaushika at the door. 'Sure, I will, please wait a little,' she replied. As soon as she completed her washing and put away the dishes, her husband came home for lunch. He was famished.

The lady was a homemaker par excellence. She was fully devoted to her role as the nourisher and caretaker of everyone in the family. When she saw her husband, as was her routine, the lady started making arrangements for his lunch. That Kaushika was waiting outside for bhikshā completely slipped her mind. It was only after she had served food to her husband that she remembered about Kaushika. A little embarrassed, she hurried to the door with the bhikshā for the Brāhmin. Kaushika had become restless by then, standing and waiting at the door.

'What kind of behaviour is this? Why did you ask me to wait if you were going to be this late? You should have just asked me to leave,' he admonished rather angrily.

'Forgive me, Sir, my husband and family have always been my foremost priority. My husband came home and was extremely hungry, and I got busy attending to him. I completely forgot that I had asked you to wait. Hence, the unfortunate delay in attending to you,' the lady responded calmly, with a tone of genuine regret.

'What? You got so busy serving your husband that you forgot about me? Is your husband's stature greater than that of a Brāhmin? Do you not know how to respect Brāhmins? Have you not heard how powerful Brāhmins are? Even Indra bows down before us,' said Kaushika, fury and arrogance palpable in his voice.

'Sir, I am not a bird who will fall dead like the one that was killed because you looked at it angrily. Let go of your anger. It will do nothing to me. I know Brāhmins well and I also respect them. I am aware of their anger and of their compassion. I really regret that

I made you wait and for that, I seek your forgiveness, even though hurting you was not my intention,' asserted the lady with her composure intact.

Then the lady continued with her wise words:

> This anger is one of the biggest enemies of humans. Only those who have controlled their anger and greed are considered Brāhmins by the wise. A person who always speaks the truth, devotedly serves his guru, shows restraint even in a situation of aggression, has gained control over his senses and mind, shows compassion towards all—humans, animals and all other living beings—is indeed a Brāhmin.
>
> I am a homemaker. Nothing else takes precedence for me than looking after the welfare of my husband and my family, not even the gods. That is my priority, my responsibility and my Dharma, and I work committedly to live by my Dharma to the best of my abilities. The result of my unflinching commitment to my Dharma is here for you to see—although I wasn't there when the bird died due to your fury, I know about the incident.
>
> The wise insist that Dharma stands on truth and forthrightness. Some suggest that Vedas are the ultimate source of Dharma. Nonetheless, subtle are the ways of Dharma. Understanding the nature of Dharma with all its nuances is not easy nor possible for everyone.
>
> Sir, you have studied the scriptures deeply and you practise austerities that they prescribe. However, I think you do not yet understand Dharma in its true essence. If you wish to learn about it, I suggest you go to the city of Mithilā and seek an audience with a meat-seller named Dharmavyādha who resides

> there. He is known to have achieved control over his senses. He serves his parents with devoutness and adheres to truth. He will certainly guide you. May you be blessed.
>
> And please do pardon me if I have said or done anything that was not appropriate. A person of virtue and learning knows the scriptural injunction that women are अवध्य (not to be killed or dishonoured).

By the time the lady concluded her erudite response, Kaushika's anger had subsided. 'Dear lady, your words are incisive and hold a lot of merit. I understand well that they will help my self-growth. Your conduct is exemplary and I will do as you say. May you be blessed,' he replied graciously. He took the bhikshā and left, feeling a little mortified at his own ignorance and impulsiveness.[3]

Dharmavyādha's Lesson on Dharma

Even after returning to his āshrama, Kaushika continued to reflect on the sagacious words of the lady and on his own conduct. 'The lady was right. I need to understand Dharma with all its subtleties for my own sake. I must take the lady's advice and see the meat-seller in Mithilā,' he thought to himself and left for Mithilā the next morning.

After several days of travelling through different towns, villages and jungles and crossing a few rivers, Kaushika finally reached Mithilā. The city was adorned with wide roads, tall arches, high-rise houses and lush green parks. He spent some time going around the city, admiring its beauty and then started looking for Dharmavyādha, the meat-seller. He asked for directions from passers-by and was guided to Dharmavyādha's shop.

Inside the shop, he saw Dharmavyādha seated at the counter, surrounded by the meat of boars and buffaloes, attending to his customers. The shop was busy at that time of the day, so Kaushika retreated into a corner and waited patiently for Dharmavyādha to finish his work.

Dharmavyādha noticed Kaushika in the crowd. He wrapped up his work quickly and approached the Brāhmin, bowing respectfully with folded hands and said, 'Welcome to Mithilā, Sir. I am indeed the meat-seller you have come looking for. I am aware that a lady of immaculate conduct suggested to you to come here. Please tell me how I may help you.'

Kaushika was perplexed. First, the lady and now this meat-seller seemed to have some sort of a psychic power which he had not yet achieved. But before he could reply, the meat-seller looked around and spoke again, 'I think this place is not suitable for you to sit and talk. If it is agreeable to you, we can go to my house and chat.'

Kaushika agreed readily and they walked towards the meat-seller's house. The house was neat and pleasant. Dharmavyādha invited the Brāhmin inside with reverence and offered him a seat and water. Kaushika accepted the hospitality. Having made himself comfortable, he asked candidly, 'Why do you sell meat? It isn't a desirable thing to do, certainly not for someone like you. I find even the thought of you sitting in your shop, surrounded by animal flesh, disgusting.'

Virtuous Conduct

Dharmavyādha smiled understandingly. He responded thoughtfully but unapologetically.

> Sir, selling meat is my profession. My ancestors were meat-sellers. I took over the responsibility from them to continue our hereditary profession. Meat selling is just another profession, like farming, trading, cattle rearing, teaching, conducting rituals and administration.

Dharmavyādha then explained to Kaushika how he strove to conduct himself.

> I am committed to my work and I do it with utmost reverence and honesty. Along with managing the demands of my profession, I also serve my old parents with dedication. I speak no falsehood, make donations according to my capacity, worship our gods, attend to guests and look after my family as well as those who work for me with utmost sincerity. I eat only after having provided for all of them. I do not talk ill of anyone, nor do I get into unnecessary conflicts with those more powerful than me. Moreover, I do not eat meat, nor do I hunt animals myself.
>
> Irrespective of the profession, a person must strive to live a life of virtue by feeding the hungry, showing respect to the respectworthy, speaking and conducting oneself truthfully, not harming anyone, achieving control over the impulses of anger, lust,

greed, jealousy and ego, and helping others even when not asked. Developing equanimity towards both joy and sorrow is critical, so is not giving up on your responsibilities, whatever may be the challenges. It is also important to engage yourself in activities that lead to personal and social well-being. And while doing this, if you commit a mistake, it is important to become aware of it, acknowledge it, take corrective actions and not repeat it. If you believe that you can convince others and yourself of your innocence after committing an act of sin, you are surely mistaken. Because in your heart you always know, there is no fooling the divine witness within yourself.

Kaushika listened in awe. 'How can I learn and imbibe such शिष्टाचार (virtuous conduct) that you just described?' he asked.

Characteristics of People of Good Conduct

Dharmavyādha expounded on the principles of good conduct. 'Let me share with you what I have learnt and what I have understood. People who exemplify virtuous conduct display some distinct characteristics:

- They have successfully conquered the impulses of anger, lust, greed, deceit, dishonesty, jealousy and tendency of fault-finding in others. They display qualities of forgiveness, satisfaction, pleasant speech and composure.
- They walk firmly on the path of their Dharma, fulfilling their various responsibilities. They find contentment in what they do.

- They follow a disciplined life, engaging in rituals prescribed by the scriptures, such as conducting yagna, studying the scriptures, practising austerities, giving donations and being firm on truthfulness.
- They do not allow their minds to even contemplate actions that are proscribed and should not be done.
- They respect and follow persons who have shown such qualities in their behaviour.
- They never give up learning and studying different kinds of arts and sciences, have faith in the divine, periodically undertake pilgrimages to sacred places, are forthright and honest in their social interactions, harbour compassion towards all beings and practise non-violence (in speech, actions and thoughts).
- They are inherently inclined towards justice and righteousness and harbour no ill will or hatred against anyone, not even those who have caused them pain.

Such people are well aware of the consequences of both good and bad actions. They constantly meditate on ways to live a just and fruitful life in accordance with Dharma. Truth is the essence of the Vedas; the essence of truth is the control of senses—indriya nigraha, the essence of indriya nigraha is the ability to let go. Such renunciation is evinced in the behaviour of people who exemplify virtuous conduct.

It is through such conduct, rooted in the wisdom of the scriptures and deep study of human actions and behaviours, both good and bad, that such people live a life in accordance with Dharma, liberated from worldly insecurities and fear.'[4]

Unpacking Violence and Non-violence

Dharmavyādha then delved even deeper into the subtlety of Dharma. He said:

> Your belief that my profession is cruel is not completely misplaced. Nonetheless, I am following a profession perfectly acceptable to the society, and one that was followed by my ancestors, one that provides me with livelihood. Even while doing so, I always contemplate ways to atone for the violence happening at my hands and live a life of humility, truthfulness and righteousness, although I am only an instrument in this act of violence because whoever is born is bound to die at some point.
>
> Undoubtedly, I would have preferred that the animals whose meat I sell were alive and used for other activities than being eaten. But we have also seen that from time immemorial, medicinal herbs, grains, grass, creepers, animals and birds have been consumed by living creatures. Some believe agriculture is a better profession. But when the land is ploughed for farming, innumerable creatures living below the soil are killed. Moreover, the seeds sown of grains are also sentient beings. Isn't violence happening there too?
>
> Many people enjoy hunting animals for fun and for food. Many others cut trees and herbs for their consumption. So many living creatures residing in the trees, plants and fruits get killed in the process. We have seen in nature that living beings depend on

other living beings for their survival. Fish eat fish. And many animals subsist on other animals.

Not just that, even while walking, sitting and sleeping, we end up killing numerous living creatures, knowingly or unknowingly. What do you think about violence inflicted by such actions?

After deep deliberation, I have arrived at the conclusion that no one, not even those who actively pursue the goal of non-violence, can be completely free of violence of some kind or the other. Nevertheless, wise people have exhorted us to practise non-violence and that is indeed an admirable pursuit. But that exhortation has to be understood in the right context and we must continuously strive to reduce violence as much as possible while engaging honestly in our profession. A person behaving thus certainly attains glory.[5]

Dharmavyādha's stress on the 'profession of ancestors' was because in ancient times it was not just considered honourable but also desirable to continue the legacy of the family. All systems were designed around the jāti–varna system. Children taking up the profession of parents is not uncommon even today, though now it is largely driven by economics and considerations of continuity of business, rather than any distinct jāti–varna consciousness. The discourse of Dharmavyādha is not about encouraging killing of animals. If meat is consumed by the society, it is futile, even hypocritical, to condemn the professions related to the meat supply chain. The idea being conveyed here, however, is more profound. It upholds the dignity of all socially accepted professions that people engage in and emphasises that virtue is not in the *kind* of profession but *how* the professional conducts himself, both in the work he does and outside of it.

Dharmavyādha paused briefly to ensure Kaushika had absorbed the gravity of the point he was making before continuing his homily on the subtle intricacies of Dharma.

> Some people say that Dharma is only that which is defined by the Vedas. Even so, Dharma has many nuances. For instance, speaking truth is paramount; truth is one of the pillars on which Dharma stands. But in situations where an innocent life is in danger or there is fear of someone losing everything or in a relationship, it is better to utter a lie if it protects than say a truth that destroys. In such scenarios, apparent truth has the impact of falsehood and apparent falsehood is in essence the truth.

Truth is that which leads to the larger good. That which causes pain and destruction is untruth. Understanding this nuance is critical for understanding the essence of Dharma.

Metaphysics of Karma

Then Dharmavyādha shared his reflections on karma (actions) and karma phala (consequences). He stated unequivocally:

> Whatever action a person does, whether good or bad, he will certainly bear its consequences. This is a fact. Many foolish people, when faced with trouble, blame the gods for their misery, but they forget that what we get in life is a result of our own past actions, good or bad. It is often seen that people born in the same nakshastra (star) have vastly different lives. This is due to the difference in their sanchit karmas[6] of their previous lives and this life. We must remember, as our scriptures tell us, that this body is impermanent and mortal but our jivātmā is permanent and indestructible. It carries our non-fructified karmas from one birth to another.

'How is the jivātmā eternal? I want to know more about this,' said Kaushika. The discussion turned towards deeper metaphysical topics such as re-birth based on pāpa–punya, working of the mind, the senses, the pancha mahābhutas (the five basic elements—sky/space, earth, water, fire and air), the gunas (sattva, rajas, tamas), creation of beings and so on. Dharmavyādha briefly explained the philosophy of Sānkhya and the approach to attaining the supreme bliss. One important message of his discourse was:

> The way to get out of this cycle of birth and death is by staying committed to your Dharma—fulfilling all personal, familial and social responsibilities righteously and developing a sense of detachment towards all worldly objects, even while partaking in them physically, by engaging the mind in the pursuit of moksha. It is only through disciplining of mind and senses and truthfulness can a person achieve supreme bliss.[7]

He summed up his discourse with some behavioural tips:

- Eat in moderation.
- Meditate on the divine before sleeping and immediately after waking up.
- Rein in greed and anger.
- Protect your austere practices by controlling your anger, protect your Dharma by not giving in to jealousy, protect your knowledge from pride and yourself by following caution.
- Practise non-violence towards all beings. Be friendly towards all. Harbour no enmity with anyone.
- Give up possessiveness. Learn to remain content in all situations.
- Kindness towards all is the greatest Dharma, forgiveness is the greatest strength. No knowledge is superior to the knowledge of self and the greatest vow is the vow of truthfulness.
- True speech is always beneficial. Only true knowledge is helpful. Only that which benefits all is truth.
- A person who does work for the sake of work without being tied down by expectations and desires is a person of wisdom and a true renunciate.
- With your heart focused on the supreme state of being, control your mind and senses with your intellect, and do not engage in objects that evoke desire.

'Only the person who gives up desire for both joy and sorrow and cultivates equanimity towards both of them achieves that supreme state of bliss,' concluded Dharmavyādha.[8]

Dharma in Action

Kaushika was awestruck at the depth and breadth of Dharmavyādha's wisdom. 'You seem to know all that is worth knowing about Dharma,' he said.

Dharmavyādha smiled. 'Let me now tell you what has made it possible for me to gain this knowledge. Come inside and meet my parents.' Kaushika saw that Dharmavyādha's parents were old, but they looked happy and comfortable. Their faces lit up on seeing their son. They blessed him wholeheartedly. The pride and joy of being his parents were visible on their faces. Kaushika was touched by the warmth the meat-seller shared with his parents.

Dharmavyādha introduced Kaushika to his parents, and they exchanged some pleasantries. Then the two resumed their conversation.

> The reason I stand here sharing wisdom with you is because of the blessings of my parents. For me, they are the gods. As I behave towards the gods, I behave towards them. I fulfil all my responsibilities towards them. I show no lethargy in serving them. I strive to keep them happy and comfortable, and so do my wife and children. I speak only what is agreeable to them and do nothing that may cause them grief. For their happiness, I will not flinch from undertaking even a task that is not prescribed. According to our Sanātana Dharma, there are five gurus—mother, father, teacher, fire and god. It is stated unequivocally that a person who serves his parents with respect and dedication will definitely lead a life of fulfilment. It was only because I was steadfast in my service towards my parents that I could have the foreknowledge about your arrival.[9]

> I can see why you have not been able to imbibe the wisdom of the scriptures despite studying them for all these years. Not only did you abandon your responsibilities towards your parents, but you also did not seek their permission before choosing this path of apparent renunciation. You disregarded their wishes and left home without even telling them. Your behaviour has caused your old parents profound sorrow. They have become nearly blind crying for you. But all is not lost yet. They continue to wait eagerly for you, hoping to see you one day. I would advise you to return to your parents and serve them in their old age as a son should.[10]

Kaushika was gratified. His trip to Mithilā had been extremely fruitful. 'I am undoubtedly fortunate to have met you and to have learnt such valuable lessons from you. I had fallen into a deep abyss but you saved me. I will surely act on your advice. I will go home and serve my parents,' promised Kaushika. He took Dharmavyādha's leave and went straight home to his parents.

> Living a life of Dharma does not require a person to go and live in forests or undertake severe penance. The requirement is simpler—fulfil your responsibilities towards your family and towards all those who are dependent on you. And whatever you do, do it with utmost commitment and honesty—that is Dharma. Both the lady and Dharmavyādha had imbibed the essence of Dharma. They lead by example by living their lives in accordance with Dharma.

ॐ

Part 6

Yaksha Prashna: Yaksha's Challenge to Yudhishthira

On seeing his brothers lying unconscious by the bank of the lake, Yudhishthira was distraught. He could not believe there was a being so powerful who was capable of defeating warriors like Arjuna and Bheema. It did not take long for him to find out who that was.

As he bent down to drink water from the lake, he heard a voice that cautioned him from drinking the water. 'I am Yaksha. I rule over this lake. Answer my questions if you wish to drink this water. Your brothers did not listen and see what has happened to them,' the voice said. Yudhishthira stopped trying to drink the water and humbly agreed to answer the questions.

Yaksha's questions tested Yudhishthira's knowledge of the scriptures as well as his wisdom and discretion. There were even some riddles. The conversation is a testimony of Yudhishthira's astute understanding of Dharma and life.[1]

The questions here are Yaksha's and responses are Yudhishthira's. The questions were asked in sets of 2–4 questions and have been split here for better reading.

- How does a person become a shrotriya[2]?
  - A person can become a shrotriya by studying the Vedas.
- How is greatness achieved?
  - Greatness is achieved by taking up a resolution and adhering to it with discipline and commitment.[3]
- How does a person get lasting companionship?
  - A person gets lasting companionship by being loyal and faithful.[4]

- How does a person become wise?
  - By serving the elderly and those with more experience and wisdom, a person can become wise.

- What is of divine importance to the Brāhmins?
  - Ceaseless study of the Vedas is of divine importance to the Brāhmins.
- What is their noble Dharma?
  - Performing austerities is their noble Dharma.
- What is their human-like tendency?
  - Death is one human-like tendency they show.
- What kind of behaviour if done by them is wicked?
  - Speaking ill about others and criticising others, if done by them, is wicked behaviour.

- What is of divine importance to the warriors (Kshatriyas)?
  - Warfare skills are of divine importance for the Kshatriyas.
- What is their Dharma?
  - Conducting yagnas is their noble Dharma.
- What is their human-like tendency?
  - Fear is their human-like tendency.
- What kind of behaviour if done by them is wicked?
  - Abandoning the needy who seek their shelter, if done by them, is wicked behaviour.

- What kind of a person who breathes, has intelligence and is also well known but is as good as dead?
  - The person who does not serve the Devas, guests, ancestors, family members and does

not nourish his own ātmā is as good as dead, even if alive.

- ✦ Who is greater and more valuable than the earth?
  – Mother is greater and more valuable than the earth.
- ✦ Who is taller than the sky?
  – Father is taller in stature than the sky.
- ✦ What is faster than the wind?
  – The mind is faster than the wind.
- ✦ What is more prolific than grass?
  – Worry is more prolific than the grass.

- ✦ What doesn't close its eyes even when asleep?
  – A fish doesn't close its eyes even when asleep.
- ✦ What doesn't show any movement even after being birthed?
  – An egg doesn't show any movement even after being birthed.
- ✦ What doesn't have a heart?
  – A stone doesn't have a heart.
- ✦ What grows bigger with speed?
  – Rivers grow bigger with speed.

- ✦ Who is the friend of a traveller?
  – Fellow travellers are friends of a traveller.
- ✦ Who is the friend of a householder?
  – A wife is the friend of a householder.
- ✦ Who is the friend of the unwell?
  – A doctor is a friend of the unwell.
- ✦ Who is the friend of the person who is about to die?
  – Charity is the friend of the person who is about to die.

- What always travels alone?
  - Sun always travels alone.
- What takes birth again and again?
  - Moon takes birth again and again.
- What is the medicine for cold?
  - Fire is the medicine for cold.
- Which is the greatest sowing field?
  - The earth is the greatest sowing field.

- What is the foundation of Dharma?
  - Enterprise is the foundation of Dharma.
- What is the source of glory?
  - Charity is the source of glory.
- What is the basis of heaven?
  - Truth is the basis of heaven.
- What is the source of happiness?
  - Character is the source of happiness.

- What is the ātmā of a human being?
  - A child is the ātmā of a human being.
- Who is a god-sent friend?
  - A spouse is a god-sent friend.
- What is it that upholds life?
  - Rain upholds life.
- What is the ultimate refuge?
  - Charity is the ultimate refuge.

- Who is the best amongst the wealthy?
  - Amongst the wealthy, those who are enterprising are the best.
- What is the best kind of wealth?
  - Knowledge of the Vedas is the best wealth.

- What is worth gaining?
  – Good health is worth gaining.
- Who is the happiest amongst all?
  – A contented person is the happiest.

- What is the foremost Dharma?
  – Compassion is the foremost Dharma.
- What action always yields results?
  – Practice of Dharma as prescribed by the Vedas always yields results.
- Controlling what does a person not repent?
  – A person does not repent controlling the mind.
- Alliance with whom doesn't wither?
  – Alliance with noble people doesn't wither.

- Giving up what endears a person?
  – Giving up pride endears a person.
- Renouncing what does a person not grieve?
  – A person does not grieve renouncing anger.
- Giving up what makes a person prosperous?
  – Giving up unwanted desires makes a person prosperous.
- Giving up what makes a person happy?
  – Giving up greed makes a person happy.

- What is it that which covers the world?
  – Ignorance covers the world.
- What stops the illumination of the world?
  – Tamas[5] stops it from illumination.
- What makes people lose friends?
  – Greed makes people lose friends.

- What stops people from going to heaven after their death?
  - Intense attachment to worldly affairs stops people from going to heaven.

- When is a person considered to be dead?
  - A person in extreme poverty is as good as dead.
- When is a country considered to be dead?
  - A country in anarchy is as good as dead.
- When is shrādha[6] considered dead (futile)?
  - A shrādha ritual conducted without a shrotriya is futile.
- When is a yagna considered dead (fruitless)?
  - Yagna done without making donations is futile.

- What is the best austerity?
  - Readily doing one's duty is the best austerity.
- What is self-restraint[7]?
  - Restraining the mind is self-restraint.
- What is the foremost form of forgiveness?
  - Developing tolerance for and endurance of dualities such as joy and sorrow, heat and cold and so on is foremost forgiveness.
- What is the meaning of 'to maintain a sense of shame'[8]?
  - Keeping away from that which shouldn't be done is to maintain a sense of shame.

- What is real knowledge?
  - The knowledge of the essence of God is real knowledge.
- What is equanimity[9]?
  - Equanimity is tranquillity of mind.

- What is compassion?
  - Desiring the well-being of all is compassion.
- What is forthrightness?
  - Even-mindedness[10] towards all is forthrightness.

- Who is the biggest enemy of a person?
  - Anger is a person's biggest enemy.
- What disease has no cure?
  - Greed has no cure.
- Who is a noble person?
  - A person who desires the well-being of all is a noble person.
- And who isn't?
  - A person who has no mercy or compassion is not a noble person.

- What is ignorance[11]?
  - Not knowing Dharma is ignorance.
- What is pride?
  - Self-conceit is pride.
- What is lethargy?
  - Not doing your duty is lethargy.
- What is grief?
  - Ignorance of true knowledge is grief.

- What according to the rishis is stability?
  - Rishis call doing your duties while being established in your swadharma as stability.
- How is fortitude[12] defined?
  - Indriya nigraha—achieving control over senses is fortitude.
- What is the best kind of ablution?

   - Cleansing the dirt of the mind is the best kind of ablution.
- What is called charity?
   - Protection of all beings is called charity[13].

- Who is to be known as a pandit?
   - A person who understands Dharma is a pandit.
- Who is called a nāstika (non-believer)? Who is a fool?
   - A fool is a non-believer and a non-believer is a fool.
- What is kāma (desire)?
   - That which is the cause of this never-ending cycle of birth and death is kāma (desire).
- What is jealousy?
   - That which causes heart burn is jealousy.

- What is arrogance (ego)?
   - Arrogance is great ignorance.
- What is deceit[14]?
   - Big talk of Dharma but hypocrisy in actual practice is deceit.
- What is called the ultimate destiny?
   - The fruit of well-intentioned charity is the ultimate destiny.
- What is slander or calumny?
   - Maligning others is calumny.

- Dharma–artha–kāma are usually seen as mutually antagonistic. How can these be brought together?
   - When a person has a spouse aligned with him in his Dharma (that is, one who supports and

facilitates the spouse in fulfilling his duties and responsibilities), Dharma, artha and kāma come together very easily.

- What kind of person is condemned to hell eternally?
  - A person who himself invites a destitute monk promising bhikshā but later denies giving, saying he has nothing to give, is condemned to eternal hell.
  - A miser who, despite having the resources, gives neither charity nor spends it for the well-being of himself and the people dependent on him, saying he has nothing, is condemned to eternal hell.
  - A person who attributes falsehood to the Vedas, Dharmashāstras and gods is condemned to everlasting hell.

- When is a person to be considered a Brāhmin—by birth, conduct, education or listening to scriptures?
  - Not by birth, not by education, not by listening to scriptures does a person become a Brāhmin. Only by virtuous conduct can a person be considered a Brāhmin. Hence, one must focus on his conduct.

- What does a person who has a sweet speech gain?
  - A person with a sweet speech endears all.
- What does a person who acts only after proper deliberation and caution gain?

  - A person who acts with caution and only after proper deliberation increases his chances of success.
- What is the gain for a person who has many friends?
  - A person with many friends lives in joy.
- What does a person who is engrossed in his duties gain?
  - A person engrossed in his duties achieves bliss in this world and the next.

- Who is truly happy?
  - A person who is not indebted to anyone, not away in a foreign land and eats food in the fifth or sixth part of the day cooked in his own house, even if with scanty vegetables, is truly happy.
- What is most astonishing?
  - Every day in the world numerous beings die, but those who are alive desire to live forever. What could be more astonishing than this?
- What is the right path?
  - Wise people have differing opinions; logic can also lead to multiple conclusions. Scriptures too have contradictory indications. The right path then is to take that which was taken by noble people.
- What information is worth having?
  - The only information worth having is this—time is cooking us all in the pan of this delusional world, with a ladle of months and seasons, on the fire of the sun, fuelled by night and day.

- How long is a person known to exist?
  - As long as a person's virtuous actions are known in the world, he is known to truly exist.
- Who is sarvadhani—one who has all kinds of wealth?
  - A person who is free of dualities and maintains his equanimity in all situations—happiness and sorrow, pleasure and pain—has all kinds of wealth.

Yaksha was satisfied with Yudhishthira's responses. He not only revived the other four Pāndavas but also revealed his identity as Dharma, the actual biological father of Yudhishthira.

ॐ

Part 7

Swargārohana: The Ascent to Heaven

Thirty-six years after the Kurukshetra war, tragedy had struck the Vrishnis of Dwarkā. Most Vrishni men had killed one another in a drunken brawl. Krishna and Balarāma had given up their bodies. The sea had engulfed Dwarkā, which was once the majestic city of the Yādavas. Some women and children who survived the deluge due to Arjuna's timely arrival and evacuation fell prey to dacoits en route to Hastināpur. Never before had Arjuna been humbled in a fight like he was by these dacoits.

All omens indicated that it was time for the Pāndavas to relinquish their power and the kingdom. Yudhishthira made Parikshita, the son of Abhimanyu and Uttarā and grandson of Arjuna and Subhadrā, the king of Hastināpur. He crowned Vraja, the surviving grandson of Krishna, the king of Indraprastha. The Pāndavas and Draupadi left Hastināpur to spend their last days in the forests.

They spent many days walking through forests, fields, hillocks and finally reached the Himālayas. They continued their walk, crossed over the snowcapped peaks of the Himālayas and finally arrived at the base of the Meru mountain. From here, their steep climb upward was to begin. They prepared themselves for the climb by regulating their breathing using techniques of yoga and began their ascent.

After a few hours, suddenly Draupadi lost her balance and fell off the cliff, dead. The brothers were shocked. They stood there watching helplessly. Distraught, Bheema asked Yudhishthira, 'Our wife Draupadi was a noble lady of great virtues. Why then did she fall off the mountain?'

'Though she loved us all, she was always biased towards Arjuna,' said Yudhishthira calmly and began climbing again. The brothers followed in silence. After having walked some distance, Sahadeva fell and lay dead in the valley below. Once again, a shaken Bheema asked Yudhishthira the reason for his fall.

'Sahadeva was very proud of his wisdom. He considered everyone else inferior to him in knowledge,' replied Yudhishthira and continued climbing. So did the others. Going a little further, they heard a loud thud. This time Nakula had fallen. 'Why him?' asked Bheema.

'Nakula's flaw was his arrogance about his good looks,' said Yudhishthira as he walked on. Next fell Arjuna. 'How can Arjuna fall? He was the best warrior amongst all,' sighed Bheema.

'Arjuna was very proud of his valour. Before the war, he had proclaimed he would kill all enemies in a day. But he didn't do so.'

The climb continued. As Bheema grieved the loss of his brothers, he slipped and fell too. Yudhishthira heard him fall but he continued his climb. Bheema wasn't dead yet. 'Why did I fall? I was devoted to you, and I know I was dear to you too,' he shouted after Yudhishthira.

'You, Bheema, were a glutton and you often praised your own self because of your strength, disregarding others,' responded Yudhishthira and continued walking. Bheema passed away soon afterwards.

Yudhishthira continued his climb. His brothers and dear wife were not there to keep him company, yet he wasn't completely alone. Since they had started the ascent, Yudhishthira had noticed that a dog had been following them. The dog had seen the fall of the brothers and Draupadi. But not for a moment had it left Yudhishthira's side.

Yudhishthira walked and walked and the dog walked with him. Then one day, Indra's chariot descended from heaven. Indra deva had himself come to take Yudhishthira. 'Get on this chariot and come with me to heaven,' said Indra.

Yudhishthira, who had maintained a calm disposition till then, couldn't hold back his grief any longer. 'Indra deva, my brothers and Draupadi lie fallen here. How can I go to heaven leaving them here? I will go only if they can come with us,' he said sorrowfully.

'Don't worry, your brothers and Draupadi are already in heaven. They gave up their earthly bodies and ascended to heaven like human beings are meant to. For you, an exception has been made. I have come to take you to heaven in this very body. Come along,' said Indra.

Yudhishthira felt greatly relieved, but there was one more being he couldn't leave. 'This dog has been my loyal companion all this while. I'd happily come if we could take him along,' he said.

Indra looked surprised, 'There is no place for a dog in heaven. In fact, if the offering made for a yagna is touched by a dog, it is considered impure. We can't possibly take the dog. The riches and pleasures of heaven await you. Not taking the dog along is not important. Don't worry and come with me.'

'There is no way I can leave someone who has been my constant companion and has been in my protection. This dog hasn't left my side since we started walking. I do not wish for the pleasures of heaven if that necessitates me to leave this dog. Deserting those who are your companions or dependent on you and look up to you is as grave a sin as destroying a foetus or killing that which the scriptures prohibit,' asserted Yudhishthira.

As soon as Yudhishthira said this, the dog disappeared and in its place appeared the lord of Dharma, Yudhishthira's biological father, the same Dharma who had tested him as Yaksha during their days in the forest. 'You are indeed an embodiment of Dharma. I am pleased with your principled stand on not leaving a loyal companion, even if it's a dog. The riches of heaven couldn't sway you from the path of Dharma,' he said, looking pleased.

They all got into their respective chariots and ascended to heaven.

On reaching heaven, Yudhishthira enquired about his brothers, Draupadi, Drishtadyumna, Sātyaki, Shikhandi as well as his other kith and kin. He also enquired about Karna. But he received no answer. He was led to a luxurious assembly hall where he saw Duryodhana sitting amongst other Devatās on an ornate throne and enjoying the pleasures of heaven.

Yudhishthira was shocked. 'How is it that Duryodhana, the person responsible for the Kurukshetra war, the one who led to the destruction of two generations of warriors and innumerable animals, get a place in heaven? Not only is he responsible for the devastation but also the humiliation of Draupadi in the Hastināpur assembly. I do not wish to see him nor speak to him. I wish to go where my brothers, other noble warriors and Draupadi are. Why don't I see them?' he asked a little rattled.

Nārada muni, who was standing nearby, smiled understandingly. 'Duryodhana died fighting as a warrior should on the battlefield. He did not fear nor flinch even though his entire army was decimated and faced the opponents courageously. He is here as a result of that. And now you are in heaven. The happenings of earth have no bearing here. Therefore, harbour no ill will towards Duryodhana,' he advised.

Yudhishthira insisted on seeing his brethren. The guards led him down a dark, narrow alley. It was hot and dusty. An intense foul smell hit Yudhishthira as he walked down the alley. He felt sick but continued to follow the guards. He could smell burnt and rotting flesh all around. The place was infested with flies, mosquitoes and all sorts of insects. As he walked further, he saw tortured dead bodies, skeletons, bones and broken limbs strewn around. He saw vultures and crows having a field day feasting over the rotting flesh.

The alley opened into a large field, equally obnoxious, but there was more. He could see various chambers. Some had pits of burning sand, some had huge pans filled with boiling oil, while some others had huge iron boulders. There were also forests where swords had replaced trees. He saw people being subjected to unspeakable torture in those chambers. He could hear their voices, screeching and screaming. He was told these beings had committed heinous sins during their life on earth.

Yudhishthira was becoming anxious about where he was being taken. 'How far do we have to go and where are my brothers?' he asked. 'We can return whenever you wish. We have been ordered to bring you back when you are tired,' the guards told him. Yudhishthira was feeling giddy. He had just seen hell and couldn't take it any more. He was about to tell the guards to take him back when he heard some familiar voices. 'You seem to have come as a breath of fresh air for us. Do not leave us and go,' the voices implored. To his utter shock, he realised that the voices were of his own people—his brothers, Draupadi, his sons and his allies.

Yudhishthira's heart was in pain on seeing his people in such a horrible condition. 'What have they done to deserve such pain? I don't remember any sin that any of them has ever committed. And Duryodhana, who lived a life of sin, has been bestowed with the pleasures of heaven. What kind of divine justice is this?' His mind was spinning with such questions. So he decided not to return to heaven. 'You people can go back to where we came from. I will stay here with my people. If they deserve to be here, I will stay here too,' he told the guards.

As soon as Yudhishthira spoke these words, Indra, Dharma and all other deities appeared before him. Miraculously, the darkness disappeared and a sweet smell filled the air. In the blink of an eye, the entire scene changed from abomination to resplendence. To Yudhishthira, it seemed as if he had woken up from a nightmare.

Indra deva's words transported him back to the present moment. 'Relax Yudhishthira,' Indra deva said. 'Don't worry over what you just experienced. Your karma has earned you a place in heaven. You had to undergo a momentary experience of hell. All kings, however great, have to go through this experience in some measure. People accumulate two kinds of karma, based on their good and bad actions. One doesn't cancel out the other. Hence, even if one kind of karma is significantly more, the consequences of the other karma have to be borne. If the good dominates, the person first faces the fruits of the not-so-good actions briefly before enjoying the fruits of the good karma.'

Indra continued, 'Likewise for the one who commits heinous sins. He has to live in hell until the karma is not expended, but before that, he does get to see heaven briefly for the little good karma he may have accumulated. That is why you saw Duryodhana enjoy the riches of heaven before he is dispatched to where his karma deserves him to be.'

Indra added, 'You misled Dronāchārya by a half-lie of elephant Ashwatthamā's death. That karma had to be paid for. You have now gone through this brief experience of hell. Just like you, your brothers and Draupadi went through this fleeting experience of the pain of hell. But it is behind all of you now. You have rightly earned your place in heaven and will live here henceforth, along with your brothers, Draupadi, sons and friends.'

After Indra, Lord Dharma spoke, his eyes shining with pride like only a father's can over his son's achievements. 'Yudhishthira, I am extremely pleased with your innate inclination towards Dharma in every situation, your truthfulness and self-restraint. I've tested you thrice now. First as Yaksha in the forest, then as a dog and a third time now. You were given a choice to return from the hellish experience, but you chose to embrace the pain of hell when you learnt that your near and dear ones were there. You were willing to live through hell if that was what was ordained for your people. Your compassion, understanding of Dharma and steadfastness in Dharma are exemplary. Your conduct has given me immense satisfaction.'

As advised by Dharma and Indra, Yudhishthira took a plunge into the celestial river and gave up his earthly body. He was taken to the place where the other Pāndavas and Draupadi had already reached. His heart was filled with joy to see his dear wife Draupadi, who sat there in all her radiance as an embodiment of Devi Lakshmi herself. He saw his brothers Bheema, Nakula and Sahadeva amongst the celestial Devas. He saw Abhimanyu and his other sons. He saw Karna, Bhishma, Dronāchārya and other relatives.

And then, as he looked beyond, he saw Krishna, not as the cousin he knew on earth, but as Nārāyana himself, lustrous and splendid. The light of his divine aura seemed to envelop everything around and beyond. Standing before Krishna was Arjuna, the Nara, immersed in the worship of Nārāyana.

'As long as a person's glory is known in the world, they continue to enjoy heaven,' the scriptures state. The story of the Kauravas and Pāndavas continues to fascinate and teach us lessons of life even today, and they continue to reside in the worlds beyond, some in heaven and some in hell, wherever their karma led them.

And Krishna—what to say of Krishna?
When was he not, where is he not, what is he not?
May our buddhi be illumined by his essence.
May we be drenched in his everlasting grace!

जले कृष्णः स्थले कृष्णर्कृष्णः पर्वतमस्तके ।
ज्वालामालाकुले कृष्णः सर्वं कृष्णमयं जगत् ।।[1]

ॐ

[illegible]

[illegible]

[illegible]

NOTES

PART 1: BHISHMA'S DISCOURSE FROM THE DEATHBED

1 Devas and Asuras are considered children of Rishi Kashyapa with Aditi and Diti, respectively. Hence, they are said to be stepbrothers—same father, different mothers.
2 Shānti Parva 33.24–33.33.
3 Prāyaschitta is scripturally instructed repentance.
4 Shānti Parva 33.43–33.46.
5 Shānti Parva 46.1–46.22.
6 Shānti Parva 50.37–50.38.
7 Shānti Parva 52.
8 Shānti Parva 55.
9 Shānti Parva 56 and 57.
10 The word used is शास्त्रार्थ कृतनिश्चय—To have ascertained the meaning of the shāstras.
11 Shānti Parva 57.11–57.14.
12 Shānti Parva 57.19–57.20.
13 Shānti Parva 56.14–56.16.
14 Shukrāchārya is an ancient Vedic rishi known for his astute understanding of polity, strategy and administration. He is considered as the guru of Asuras.
15 Shānti Parva 57.01–57.04.
16 Shānti Parva 57.21–57.22.
17 Shānti Parva 56.44–56.46.
18 Shānti Parva 56.19–56.21.
19 Shānti Parva 56.17–56.18.
20 Brāhaspatya—the followers of the teachings of Brihaspati, who is considered the guru of the Devatās and one of the most intelligent Devarshi ever.
21 Shānti Parva 56.35–56.40.
22 Shānti Parva 57.05–57.10.
23 Shānti Parva 56.47.

24 Shānti Parva 57.18.
25 Shānti Parva 56.29–56.21.
26 Kautilya's *Arthashāstra* 4.8.27–4.8.28, translation by R.P. Kangle.
27 Shānti Parva 57.16.
28 Shānti Parva 56.41.
29 Shānti Parva 56.48–56.61.
30 Shānti Parva 57.17.
31 Shānti Parva 57.23–57.25.
32 Shānti Parva 56.42–56.43.
33 Shānti Parva 57.30–57.39.
34 Shānti Parva 57.40–57.45.
35 Shānti Parva 58.05–58.12.
36 Shānti Parva 58.13–58.17.
37 Shānti Parva 58.18.
38 Shānti Parva 58.19–58.20.
39 Bhishma doesn't use the word 'whistleblower', but his words mean exactly this.
40 Shānti Parva 82.02–82.05.
41 Shānti Parva 58.21–58.23.
42 The shloka is सेवेत प्रणयं हित्वा—the meaning isn't conclusive as different translations have given slightly different meanings. The larger idea, though, is to serve without slighting.
43 Shānti Parva 70.
44 Shānti Parva 137.
45 Anāgatavidhātā literally means one who can know what is going to happen before it happens.
46 Pratyutpannamati literally means sharp-minded or quick-witted.
47 Deerghasutri literally means one who procrastinates.
48 Shānti Parva 59.
49 Mānasputra: One who is born out of one's mānas (mind); in another sense, it is an idea personified.
50 Shānti Parva 69.04–69.05.
51 Shānti Parva 112.19.
52 Shānti Parva 160.
53 Shānti Parva 120.18.
54 Udyoga Parva 34.59.

55 Danda is a technical term in the Saptānga framework. It refers to the security might or coercive force of the State which is essential in establishing law and order. Hence army/security forces is the term used for danda.
56 Some texts have durga (fort) as one of the Saptānga instead of puram (capital city). The two are not very different in terms of meaning as the capital city was usually situated in a fort.
57 Shānti Parva 69.64–69.65.
58 Shānti Parva 69.66–69.68.
59 Shānti Parva 69.68–69.70.
60 This topic has been covered repeatedly, in multiple chapters. This particular line, and the one in quotes spoken by Bhishma, though, have been taken from Shānti Parva 115.12–115.13.
61 Purohita was a royal priest who officiated the royal rituals and also guided the king on the path of Dharma.
62 Shānti Parva 73.01–73.02.
63 Shānti Parva 80.21–82.28.
64 Shānti Parva 71.08–71.09.
65 Shānti Parva 83.02.
66 Shānti Parva 83.06–83.07.
67 Shānti Parva 80.21–80.30, 83.03–83.20.
68 Shānti Parva 85.07–85.12.
69 Shānti Parva 83.21–83.54.
70 Shānti Parva 69.06–69.13.
71 Shānti Parva 12.37.
72 Shānti Parva 88.16–88.17.
73 Shānti Parva 88.27, 87.36–87.40.
74 Shānti Parva 71.15.
75 Shānti Parva 88.01–88.06, 88.12.
76 Shānti Parva 87.13–87.17.
77 Shānti Parva 88.29–88.30.
78 Shānti Parva 87.38–87.40.
79 Shānti Parva 88.26.
80 Shānti Parva 89.03–89.08.
81 Shānti Parva 71.16.
82 Shānti Parva 88.14–88.15, 88.21.
83 Shānti Parva 71.16, 120.35.

84 Shānti Parva 89.01.
85 Shānti Parva 71.17–71.20.
86 Shānti Parva 69.30.
87 Shānti Parva 121.11.
88 Shānti Parva 121.34–121.35.
89 Shānti Parva 88.18–88.19.
90 Shānti Parva 69.27.
91 Shānti Parva 122.40: This and the next shloka come as a part of a conversation between Mandhātā and Vasuhoma as narrated by Bhishma to Yudhishthira.
92 Shānti Parva 122.41.
93 Shānti Parva 69.28.
94 Shānti Parva 132.11.
95 Shānti Parva 69.17.
96 Shānti Parva 122.
97 'What Is "Sengol" Installed in New Parliament Building?' *India Today*, 8 September 2023, https://www.indiatoday.in/information/story/what-is-sengol-installed-in-new-parliament-building-2385482-2023-05-28; PIB Delhi, 'At the Inauguration of the New Parliament House, PM Modi Will Establish the Historical and Sacred "Sengol" in the Parliament House', *Ministry of Home Affairs*, 24 May 2023, https://pib.gov.in/PressReleasePage.aspx?PRID=1926883.
98 Shānti Parva 80.
99 Shānti Parva 103.45–103.51 until this point. The additional points are from Shānti Parva 164.
100 Shānti Parva 120.39–120.40.
101 Shānti Parva 120.42.
102 Shānti Parva 69.14–69.15.
103 Shānti Parva 69.16.
104 Shānti Parva 69.18.
105 Shānti Parva 69.19–69.20.
106 Shānti Parva 69.21–69.22.
107 Shānti Parva 69.23–69.24.
108 Shānti Parva 69.33–69.34.
109 Shānti Parva 69.35–69.62.
110 Shānti Parva 69.38.
111 Shānti Parva 69.63.

112 Shānti Parva 103.08–103.44.
113 Shānti Parva 89.9.
114 Shānti Parva 113.
115 Shānti Parva 87.01–87.11.
116 Shānti Parva 95.06–95.22, 96.
117 The word used is 'nishprāna'.
118 Shānti Parva 96.
119 Kshatriyas were allowed 'rākshasa vivāha', where, by show of power, they could abduct a maiden for marriage. But even in that case, the scriptures say that the consent of the woman matters. Hence, no force can be used on her to give her consent.
120 Shānti Parva 96.01–96.02, 96.24.
121 Shānti Parva 67.
122 Shānti Parva 109.
123 Karna Parva 69.
124 Shānti Parva 120. This chapter is a recapitulation, once again, of Rāja dharma by Bhishma on Yudhishthira's request. Some general but important points from Shānti Parva 120 have already been included in the previous chapters to make those chapters comprehensive; those have been excluded from this chapter.
125 Shānti Parva 120.04–120.07,120.16–120.17.
126 Shānti Parva 120.19–120.20.
127 Shānti Parva 120.25, 120.30.
128 Shānti Parva 120.51–120.52.
129 Shānti Parva 130.01–130.12.
130 Shānti Parva 130.13–130.42, 133.02–133.06.
131 Shānti Parva 136.
132 Shānti Parva 131.
133 Shānti Parva 138.
134 Shānti Parva 134.01–134.08.
135 Shānti Parva 133.13–133.17.
136 Yudhishthira asked this question in relation to changing yugas, from Tretā to Dwāpar to Kali. But the advice is valid within the yugas too, as change affects everything.
137 Shānti Parva 140.
138 Shānti Parva 134.12–134.15.
139 Shānti Parva 141.

140 Shānti Parva 142.
141 I have covered important parts of that discussion in the section 'Indriya Nigraha' and hence I am not repeating it here.
142 Shānti Parva 163.
143 Vana Parva 135–137.
144 Shānti Parva 180.
145 This is a very well-known Sanskrit phrase. The source text of the phrase is unknown.
146 Anushāsana Parva 1.
147 Kāla is time. Shiva is called Mahākāla—the one who is beyond time and controls time.
148 Anushāsana Parva 6.
149 Gunas: Virtues, qualities or characteristics.
150 Stotra: Hymn.
151 Anushāsana Parva 149.
152 Anushāsana Parva 17.

PART 2: NĀRADA MUNI'S ADVICE ON ADMINISTRATION

1 Sabhā Parva 5.20.
2 Ayodhyā Kānda, sarga 100.
3 This comes from *Dakshasmriti*, as mentioned in footnote 1 of Sabhā Parva 5.20 in Gitā Press's Māhābhārata Vol. 1.
4 The six attributes mentioned are व्याख्यान शक्ति, प्रगल्भता, तर्क कुशलता, भूतकाल स्मृति, भविष्य दृष्टि, नीति निपुणता.
5 Four months can be considered as 'minimum livelihood security' in today's parlance. The minimum number of months could have been suggested as four because, in those times, four months of the rainy season were days of rest and recuperation and not much economic activity took place.

PART 3: VIDURA NITI: LESSONS ON LIFE AND LIVING FROM VIDURA

1 Omens.
2 The section between Udyoga Parva 33 to 40 is Prajāgara Parva, also called *Vidura Niti*.
3 Udyoga Parva 33.16–33.29, 33.40.
4 Faith or belief.
5 Udyoga Parva 33.30–33.39.

6 As the style of messaging makes for an interesting reading, I have maintained the order of the shlokas as in the text instead of doing a theme-based grouping.
7 Udyoga Parva 33.41.
8 Udyoga Parva 33.42.
9 Udyoga Parva 33.43.
10 Udyoga Parva 33.45.
11 Udyoga Parva 33.46.
12 Udyoga Parva 33.47.
13 Udyoga Parva 33.48–33.49.
14 Udyoga Parva 33.52.
15 Udyoga Parva 33.53.
16 Udyoga Parva 33.59.
17 Udyoga Parva 33.54.
18 Udyoga Parva 33.56. The literal translation is closer to 'Desire of a poor person and anger of the powerless'.
19 Udyoga Parva 33.55.
20 Udyoga Parva 33.60. The phrase Vidura uses is 'should be drowned in water with a heavy stone tied around their neck'.
21 Udyoga Parva 33.58.
22 उञ्छवृत्ति was a type of vrata/austerity that people would undertake for a stipulated period or for the rest of their lives. They would gather and eat only the grains fallen in the fields.
23 The word used is 'prastha' which translates to 'kilo'.
24 Udyoga Parva 33.63.
25 Udyoga Parva 33.65.
26 Udyoga Parva 33.66.
27 Udyoga Parva 33.69.
28 Udyoga Parva 33.71–33.72.
29 Udyoga Parva 33.76.
30 Udyoga Parva 33.77.
31 Udyoga Parva 33.78.
32 Udyoga Parva 33.81.
33 Udyoga Parva 33.82.
34 Udyoga Parva 33.83.
35 Udyoga Parva 33.84–33.85.
36 Udyoga Parva 33.89.

37 Udyoga Parva 33.90.
38 Udyoga Parva 33.80.
39 Udyoga Parva 33.91–33.92.
40 Udyoga Parva 33.96–33.98.
41 Udyoga Parva 33.99.
42 Udyoga Parva 33.100.
43 Udyoga Parva 33.101–33.102.
44 Udyoga Parva 33.44.
45 Srikamakshi, 'Last Anuvaka of Chamakam … Significance Explained', Sri Kamakshi Community Centre, 16 November 2017, https://srikamakshi.org/2017/11/16/last-anuvaka-of-chamakam-significance-explained/.
46 Udyoga Parva 33.103–33.121.
47 Udyoga Parva 34.01–34.06.
48 Udyoga Parva 34.08–34.09.
49 'What is in it for me?' is not directly mentioned—the author has taken liberty to use a contemporary phrase for the idea propounded in the original.
50 Udyoga Parva 34.19–34.20.
51 Udyoga Parva 34.22.
52 Udyoga Parva 34.15–34.16.
53 Udyoga Parva 34.43.
54 Udyoga Parva 35.51.
55 Udyoga Parva 37.07.
56 Udyoga Parva 37.41.
57 Udyoga Parva 37.40.
58 Udyoga Parva 39.33–33.34.
59 Udyoga Parva 39.06–39.07.
60 Udyoga Parva 39.54.
61 Udyoga Parva 39.55.
62 Udyoga Parva 39.57.
63 Udyoga Parva 39.53.
64 Udyoga Parva 38.38.
65 Udyoga Parva 39.68.
66 Udyoga Parva 38.31.
67 Udyoga Parva 39.72.
68 Udyoga Parva 39.02.
69 Udyoga Parva 35.67–35.68.
70 Udyoga Parva 37.17.

71 Udyoga Parva 34.41.
72 Udyoga Parva 36.28–36.30.
73 Udyoga Parva 35.70.
74 Udyoga Parva 36.39–36.40.
75 Udyoga Parva 34.42.
76 Udyoga Parva 34.44.
77 Udyoga Parva 35.50.
78 Udyoga Parva 35.64–35.65
79 Udyoga Parva 36.44–36.45. The word used in the verse is संताप which means anguish, that is, mental agony/stress/agitation.
80 Udyoga Parva 36.42.
81 Udyoga Parva 37.47.
82 Udyoga Parva 40.04 (1/2).
83 Udyoga Parva 37.07. This shloka mentions seventeen types of fools; out of them, I have removed three to avoid distracting the readers as their context and meanings are not clear enough. The excluded ones are—engage in unrestrained jest with daughter-in-law, reside in privacy with daughter-in-law and obtain pleasure in restraining women.
84 Udyoga Parva 34.55–34.57.
85 Udyoga Parva 34.58.
86 Udyoga Parva 34.59–34.60. This analogy is explained in the sub-section 'The Chariot Analogy' in the first section of this book as well.
87 Udyoga Parva 34.61–34.62.
88 Udyoga Parva 34.64–34.65.
89 Udyoga Parva 39.40.
90 Udyoga Parva 40.24.
91 Udyoga Parva 40.22.
92 Udyoga Parva 34.32.
93 Udyoga Parva 34.33. The word used for 'gathering grains for food' is शिलाहारी. In the past, there were people who ate only the food which they had collected, grain by grain, from farms. Every grain mattered to them. Vidura uses them as an analogy and says that wisdom can be obtained from numerous places. You only have to put in the effort and keep looking and learning. Such living is also called उञ्छवृत्ति.

94 Udyoga Parva 40.04 (1/2).
95 Udyoga Parva 40.05.
96 Udyoga Parva 40.06.
97 Udyoga Parva 39.39.
98 Udyoga Parva 35.49.
99 Udyoga Parva 36.37. The actual word in the shloka for which 'acquaintances' is used is 'sangitani' which literally translates to 'companions'. However, I believe 'acquaintances' explains the purport of the shloka better in English.
100 Udyoga Parva 39.34.
101 Udyoga Parva 40.23.
102 Udyoga Parva 39.47.
103 Udyoga Parva 39.48–39.49.
104 Udyoga Parva 39.50.
105 Udyoga Parva 34.45.
106 Udyoga Parva 34.72.
107 Udyoga Parva 34.70.
108 Udyoga Parva 39.71.
109 Udyoga Parva 40.11–40.12.
110 Udyoga Parva 40.14–40.18.
111 Udyoga Parva 40.21.
112 Udyoga Parva 35.60–35.62.
113 Udyoga Parva 35.71.
114 Udyoga Parva 39.66.
115 Udyoga Parva 37.37.
116 Udyoga Parva 37.30.
117 The word used is घृणी राजा. घृणा has multiple meanings in Sanskrit. It could mean disgust and disrespect as well as compassion. Here, the former meaning makes more sense.
118 Udyoga Parva 37.35.
119 Udyoga Parva 37.36.
120 Udyoga Parva 37.57. In this dictum and a couple of other places, while advising the king to be watchful and not trust certain groups and types of people, women have been included. While on the face of it, such a message does come across as sexist or as dismissive of women, it has to be understood with consideration

to the era being spoken of. This exhortation is being made to a king, a leader, male in this context. Lust is the most common frailty in men and is easy to exploit. Even otherwise powerful and learned kings have fallen prey to it. Thus, women were routinely and effectively used as spies as well as contract killers. 'Honey trap' is a phenomenon even today and people in the armed forces as well as in jobs of national importance are routinely cautioned about interactions with women online or in person. Nonetheless, I have chosen to not include it in the list here as I believe that given the fluidity of roles today, women getting educated and taking lead roles in institutions and public life in general, the specific caution about women doesn't hold any more. That said, even in ancient times, it doesn't mean women were not trusted. We have examples from Mauryan times where women acted as bodyguards. We have examples of women like Draupadi in Mahābhārata itself who managed the finances of the kingdom.

121 Udyoga Parva 38.39.
122 Udyoga Parva 39.08.
123 Udyoga Parva 37.52–37.55.
124 Udyoga Parva 34.35–34.37.
125 Udyoga Parva 34.50–34.51.
126 Udyoga Parva 34.52.
127 Udyoga Parva 34.53.
128 Udyoga Parva 36.48.
129 Udyoga Parva 37.19.
130 Udyoga Parva 39.76.
131 Udyoga Parva 39.81.
132 Udyoga Parva 39.82.
133 Udyoga Parva 39.84.
134 Udyoga Parva 38.11.
135 Udyoga Parva 37.33.
136 Udyoga Parva 37.34.
137 Udyoga Parva 39.70.
138 Udyoga Parva 39.04.
139 Udyoga Parva 39.46. This shloka does not appear in the critical edition.

140 Udyoga Parva 34.81–34.82.
141 Udyoga Parva 34.83–34.85
142 Ādi Parva 175, 176.
143 Udyoga Parva 35.06–35.41.
144 Udyoga Parva 34.10. Danda means punishment, hence also means the state of justice delivery. Danda is also used for the army (सेना). Both are applicable here.
145 Udyoga Parva 34.11.
146 Udyoga Parva 34.12.
147 Udyoga Parva 34.30.
148 Udyoga Parva 34.25–34.26.
149 Udyoga Parva 35.58.
150 Udyoga Parva 37.15–35.16.
151 Udyoga Parva 37.22–37.26.
152 Udyoga Parva 37.51.
153 Udyoga Parva 37.38.
154 Udyoga Parva 37.27.
155 Udyoga Parva 38.16.
156 Udyoga Parva 38.15.
157 Udyoga Parva 38.18.
158 Udyoga Parva 38.19.
159 Udyoga Parva 35.44.
160 Udyoga Parva 38.25.
161 Udyoga Parva 38.26.
162 Udyoga Parva 38.29.
163 Udyoga Parva 38.32.
164 Udyoga Parva 38.37.
165 Udyoga Parva 39.36–39.38.
166 Udyoga Parva 37.56.
167 Udyoga Parva 38.08.
168 Udyoga Parva 39.75.
169 Udyoga Parva 37.29.
170 Udyoga Parva 37.09–37.11.
171 The word used for forthrightness is आर्जव.
172 Udyoga Parva 35.02–35.04.
173 Vana Parva 199.
174 Udyoga Parva 36.49–36.74.
175 Udyoga Parva 39.09.

PART 4: KĀMA GEETĀ: THE SONG OF KĀMA

1 Ashvamedhikā Parva 2.14–2,20.
2 Ashvamedhikā Parva 11.04–11.05.
3 Ashvamedhikā Parva 12.01–12.06.
4 Ashvamedhikā Parva 13.3. In Sanskrit, the word used for eternal bliss is शाश्वत which stands for that which is eternal, permanent and constant. The reference is being made to the eternal, unchanging Brahman. It doesn't mean the body doesn't die—it dies as it is supposed to. But the person who has realised the Brahman manages to rise beyond the dualities and experiences lasting peace in this world itself and is not bogged down by hindrances and miseries of life. Such a person continues to do what needs to be done, neither deterred by short-term setbacks nor overjoyed by short-term gains.
5 Ashvamedhikā Parva 13.

PART 5: VYĀDHA GEETĀ: THE SERMON OF A MEAT-SELLER

1 Vedāngas: The word literally means the limbs of the Vedas. In order to study the Vedas, the students were expected to know the limbs, that is, the Vedāngas for proper understanding of the Vedas, chanting of the shlokas and performance of the prescribed rituals. Vedāngas include Sheekshā, Chhanda, Vyākarana, Nirukta, Kalpa and Jyotisha.
2 Bhikshā: Practice followed by sādhus, sanyāsis, Hindu monks and many Brāhmins (especially in their student days) of seeking alms and food for sustenance. The idea is to subdue one's ego by seeking support for survival, as well as achieving control over the senses by the seeker while ensuring the society looked after those engaged in practices of learning and preserving Vedic wisdom.
3 Vana Parva 206.
4 Vana Parva 207.
5 Vana Parva 208.
6 Sanchit karmas: Those accumulated karmas or actions which haven't borne consequences yet.
7 Vana Parva 209.45–209.54.
8 Vana Parva 213.26–213.40.

9 Vana Parva 214.
10 Vana Parva 215.05–215.10.

PART 6: YAKSHA PRASHNA: YAKSHA'S CHALLENGE TO YUDHISHTHIRA

1 Vana Parva 313.
2 'Shrotriya' is a technical term used for one who is learned in 'Shruti', i.e., Vedas.
3 Yudhishthira uses the word तप which typically means scripturally ordained austerity that requires taking a sankalpa, i.e., a resolution and seeing the resolution to completion.
4 Yudhishthira uses the word धृति which could mean loyalty, faithfulness, resoluteness, steadfastness, patience and so on. In this context, 'loyal' and 'faithful' are the most apt here.
5 Tamas is one of the three gunas associated with prakriti (physical matter) per Sānkhya Darshan. It is a quality of inertia, darkness, ignorance, inactivity, dullness and so on.
6 Shrādha: Ritual performed to pay homage to the dead.
7 The word used is दम.
8 The word used is ह्री.
9 The word used is शम.
10 The word used is सम चित्तता.
11 The word used is मोह.
12 The word used is धैर्य.
13 The word used for 'protection of all beings' is भूतरक्षणं.
14 The word is दम्भ.

PART 7: SWARGĀROHANA: THE ASCENT TO HEAVEN

1 This verse is inspired by a verse in the Gherānda Samhita. The original has Vishnu instead of Krishna.